CHINESE HEALING FOODS and HERBS

(Previously published as Chinese Herbal Remedies by Universe Books)

草藥

CHINESE HEALING FOODS and HERBS

(Previously published as Chinese Herbal Remedies by Universe Books)

Albert Y. Leung

Drawings by Bing Fun Leung

AYSL Corporation
Glen Rock, New Jersey

Published in the United States of America
by AYSL Corporation
P.O. Box 181, Glen Rock, NJ 07452

93 94 95 96 97 / 10 9 8 7 6 5 4 3 2 1

Printed in the United States of America

Library of Congress Cataloging in Publication Data

Leung, Albert Y.
Chinese herbal remedies.

Bibliography: p.
Includes index.
1. Herbs—Therapeutic use. 2. Materia medica, Vegetable—China. 3. Medicine, Chinese—Formulae, receipts, prescriptions. 4. Medicine, Chinese—History. I. Title.
RM666.H33L48 1984 615'.321 92-97208
ISBN 0-9634979-0-1

To my wife Barbara,
and our daughters Amy and Camille

Contents

INTRODUCTION

Chinese medicine is extremely complicated. Involving more than just treating people with herbs, it represents thousands of years of Chinese empirical wisdom, as well as a way of life closely associated with Oriental philosophy.

The herbal aspect accounts for only about half the scope of Chinese medicine; the other half encompasses philosophy, nutrition, and preventive medicine, among other subjects. Chinese medicine treats the body as a whole; only occasionally does it target-shoot at a disease —a distinct contrast to most of modern Western medicine. Whether or not he gave them medicines to take, a good Chinese doctor, in treating his patients, would advise them about what to eat and what to avoid during the course of their illness. He would also advise them to adjust their life-styles in order to achieve total well-being. A typical example of this holistic approach to medicine is the treatment of that universal ailment—hemorrhoids. There are many remedies for hemorrhoids in the Chinese medicine chest, but they are not the doctor's primary recourse. The principal treatment is the adjustment of diet and living habits. Sufferers are advised not to eat greasy, fried foods and spicy dishes such as those seasoned with chili or peppers, because these are believed to aggravate the symptoms. They are instructed to eat only mild foods (e.g., steamed and boiled dishes) and get plenty of rest. Usually, with this treatment, the hemorrhoidal symptoms and discomfort subside or disappear in a few days, even without the use of herbs. But, of course, herbs are frequently used in treatment.

The drugs used in Chinese medicine currently number close to 6,000. Although derived primarily from plant sources, some of these drugs come from animal and mineral sources. From these 6,000 basic drugs, countless numbers of remedies are prepared. Most of these have been used for hundreds (some for thousands) of years. Unlike most of our modern drugs, they are not newcomers to the human scene, not laboratory-invented. They do not, as modern drugs do, require so-called long-term studies, nor do we wait anxiously to find out what kind of diseases they happen to produce as toxic side effects. These traditional Chinese remedies are time-tested to be safe, not just for a few years or a couple of decades, but for generations, centuries, and millennia. These drugs have in effect been through the trial-and-error process with human beings and not with mice, rats, or dogs. Over long periods, the toxic properties of certain drugs or remedies were noted and recorded. Some toxic ones were discarded, while others, which are still effective, have been retained along with well-documented accounts of their toxic properties. These are often accompanied by instructions on how to avoid or mitigate these effects. Aconite and nux vomica are good examples. Both drugs are highly toxic, containing respectively the deadly alkaloids aconitine and strychnine. Western medicine shuns them. In Chinese medicine, however, they are commonly used, but they are used with special precautions. To make them less toxic, other herbs are almost always prescribed along with them; frequently, as an added safety measure, hours are spent preparing the decoctions. Alternatively, sometimes a special process—actually a form of deep-frying—is used to remove most of the drugs' toxic components.

Nevertheless, it should be cautioned, poisonings as a result of misuse do occasionally occur, and have been reported in Chinese medical and pharmaceutical journals. The most common cause of such poisoning is patients' failure to follow instructions when preparing the decoctions. To save time, they boil the herbs for less than the prescribed length of time, and this may result in serious consequences. Some patients, familiar with modern scientific principles or the low esteem in which boiling is held by nutritionists, might believe that less boiling would retain more of the drugs' active principles. They might not be aware of the other purposes of this long decocting process, and would become typical illustrations of the expression "A little knowledge is a dangerous thing."

Still, although the properties of herbs should be respected, a unique feature of Chinese herbal recipes as compared to modern drugs is their relatively nontoxic nature when used properly. Furthermore, not only do they cause few or no toxic side effects, they are now being used in China to reduce the toxic side effects caused by modern drugs, especially those used in the treatment of cancer. Western medicine frowns on the use of combinations of herbs in treating diseases, yet it does not hesitate to treat them with combinations of drugs, and —in the case of cancer—with radiation as well. It appears that Western medicine is just starting to discover what Chinese medicine has already been aware of for thousands of years—that the properties of various chemicals can work together to combat disease.

The Shennong Herbal *(Shen Nong Ben Cao*),* dating from about 200 B.C., is generally considered to be the oldest Chinese herbal. The

*Throughout this book, unless otherwise indicated, the pinyin system for transliterating Chinese characters will be used. It has been chosen over the Wade-Giles system because it approximates actual Chinese pronunciation more closely than the Wade-Giles system.

information contained in this herbal is generally credited to the legendary emperor Shennong, who is said to have lived around 2700 B.C. The herbal records 365 drugs, of which 120 are considered nontoxic, another 120 mildly toxic depending on usage, and 125 toxic and not suitable for long-term use. For example, among the herbs in the nontoxic category are ginseng and licorice, while, of the drugs best known to Westerners, rhubarb and aconite are two of those in the toxic category. Most of the drugs in this herbal are still being used in Chinese medicine. It has been revised and expanded at various times to include new drug sources.

Numerous other herbals were compiled after the Shennong Herbal, some incorporating drugs of foreign, as well as Chinese, origin. The most famous of these later herbals is the *Ben Cao Gang Mu* (Herbal Systematics), by Li Shizhen, written about 1590–96. It is composed of 52 volumes and describes 1,892 drugs. This herbal, too, is still a standard reference for the traditional Chinese physician; it is also frequently consulted by researchers on Chinese medicine.

In recent years, numerous books on Chinese herbal or folk medicine have been published both inside and outside of China. Some include physical descriptions of herbs, describe their properties and uses, and provide recipes, while others are more scientific in their botanical and chemical approach and incorporate scientific data on Chinese drugs. Many of these books are extensive compilations of the knowledge relating to Chinese drugs that has been accumulated since the Shennong Herbal first appeared. The most comprehensive work to date is the *Zhong Yao Da Ci Dian* (Encyclopedia of Chinese Drugs) compiled by the Jiangsu Institute of Modern Medicine. First published in China in 1977, and reprinted in Hong Kong in 1978, it consists of three volumes, the third of which contains an extensive appendix-index. It describes in detail 5,767 traditional herbal, animal, and mineral drugs currently used in the practice of medicine throughout China. Modern (up to 1974) pharmacological, clinical, chemical, botanical, and other scientific research data from all over the world are incorporated, including the results of research in Japan, Russia, Germany, England, and the United States, as well as China itself. Judging from the standpoint of my own areas of training—botanical, chemical, and pharmaceutical—the information contained in this work is incredibly accurate and comprehensive.

Thus, a wealth of information on useful and effective medicines, spanning a period of at least 2,000 years, exists in Chinese writings. However, few Westerners are aware of this. Most of them still think of Chinese medicine as consisting of only rhinoceros horns, snake oils, acupuncture, or ginseng, to name the few well-publicized items. While some Westerners view Chinese medicine with suspicion and disdain, others have not hesitated to make money out of it. These attitudes of derision or exploitation have not helped to present Chinese medicine as a legitimate healing art to the Western world. Let us take just two examples, ginseng and acupuncture. These are as legitimate in Chinese medicine as are aspirin and surgery in Western medicine, although use of ginseng and acupuncture dates back many centuries before the use of surgery and aspirin.

In Chinese medicine, ginseng is considered a tonic, with very subtle effects that are not evident with short-term use. It does not kill bacteria as penicillin does, nor does it relieve angina attacks as nitroglycerin does. However, ginseng strengthens the body's defenses, and helps the user's total well-being—if he can afford it. The problem with ginseng in the West, especially in America, is that many of the people who sell it in prepared forms (capsules, tablets, etc.) know nothing about it, nor do they care about its quality. Since ginseng is an expensive herb and no official standards govern its quality, it is very easy for unscrupulous manufacturers to cut it with cheap inert ingredients such as sugar and starch and pass this off as genuine ginseng. Consequently, consumers of these products do not get the true benefits of ginseng, which further adds to the disrepute of Chinese medicine in the eyes of the general public. This applies as well to other Chinese herbal drugs (e.g., *dang gui* and royal jelly).

Since acupuncture was first publicized several years ago, acupuncture clinics have sprung up in Western countries. The quality of some of these clinics and their acupuncturists should be considered suspect. Acupuncture is a time-honored art learned through years of apprenticeship and practice; it is often handed down from father to son and sometimes from master to trusted disciple. The true practitioner of acupuncture is generally an erudite individual. Beware of self-proclaimed acupuncture experts who don't even read Chinese, irrespective of their other credentials. In considering Chinese medicine in general, one should recognize that there is merit in the old Chinese proverb "The medicines of a doctor in whose family medicine has not been practiced for three generations should not be taken."

Chinese medicine is one of the oldest surviving healing arts in the world that are still actively being used. It is not, like some other Old World healing arts, just a system studied and maintained by a few highly specialized, obscure scholars. Chinese herbal medicine has never waned or died, as have the healing systems of ancient Babylonia, Egypt, Greece, and India. Rather, it has been an active and ongoing aspect of Chinese civilization for several thousand years. Being a very practical people, the Chinese make do with whatever is available to them. Plants have always been one of their biggest natural resources, and the Chinese have certainly been making good use of them. No other people in the world has such a rich written record of the medicinal uses of herbs. Practically every therapeutic class of drugs can be found in these records, and they are an extremely valuable source for discovering modern drugs. European, Russian, and Japanese scientists have been actively researching these records and analyzing Chinese drugs for years. And, although latecomers, American researchers have also recently started paying serious attention to Chinese herbs. On their part, the 20th-century Chinese have integrated their traditional medicine with Western medicine, complementing one with the other. In China today, a combination of traditional and Western drugs is often used in treating various illnesses. In fact, there is a new scientific journal in China—the *Chinese Journal of Integrated Traditional and Western Medicine*—published every two months since 1980, which is specifically devoted to this aspect of medicine.

Conditions such as colds, sore throat, coughs, diarrhea, and minor virus infections normally resolve themselves within days, whether or not medicines (herbal or modern) are taken. This again shows us that our bodies are basically tough and can rid themselves of factors that cause us to be ill. In conformance with the philosophy and teachings of Chinese medicine, we all can live a healthy and long life if we do things in moderation and take good care of our bodies. Nothing is worse for a person than to indulge in smoking, drinking, or overeating and to expect modern drugs to cure the ills caused by these excesses. The opposite is often true. These modern drugs may relieve one particular condition, but they often produce other illnesses. (Particularly notorious are congenital defects caused by thalidomide and cancers of the vagina or uterine cervix in daughters of women who took DES ([diethylstilbestrol]) during their pregnancy many years earlier.) Hence, if one possibly can, one should stay away from drugs. In this respect, I agree completely with Dr. Jere Goyan, who, shortly after taking office as commissioner of the U.S. Food and Drug Administration in October 1979, said, "My general philosophy is the fewer drugs people take, the better off they are."

Nevertheless, Western culture is a drug-oriented one, and if people are going to continue to be comforted by the idea that there is something they can take for their symptoms, it is far better that they —that we all—begin to rely more on the natural food substances, such as herbs, spices, and vegetables, we normally eat or use every day. The aim of this book is to indicate how many of our kitchen-and-garden substances are the basis of Chinese medicines, among them almonds, cucumbers, dandelions, garlic, ginger, mint, black and white pepper, sunflower seeds, tea, and walnuts. Some of these medicines are recent entries—a few generations old—to the system of Chinese medicine, while most have been used for centuries.

For thousands of years, Chinese medicine has based its practice on *yin* and *yang,* a system of balance and harmony within the body.* When drugs are used in the practice of Chinese medicine, generally their purpose is to restore this balance and allow the body to cure itself. Thus, the effects of most Chinese drugs are rather subtle and are not readily explained by science. This has prompted many Western scientists to dismiss these effects as merely psychologically generated, psychosomatic, or as placebos—ideas familiar to them. They have failed to acknowledge the fact that medical researchers have become increasingly aware of the ability of the body under certain conditions to produce its own chemicals, or "drugs," to combat diseases and illness. We all know that adrenaline can make us perform feats we would never dream of performing under ordinary circumstances. It is also known that the mind can trigger the brain to produce pain killers, called endorphins, more powerful than morphine, and that the body can produce prostaglandins and interferons under various conditions. These chemicals, especially interferons, are now highly touted, and considered by some pharmaceutical and medical researchers as virtual cure-alls. Yet these same researchers generally go out of their way to ignore the psychosomatic aspect of drugs. The possibility that some seemingly inert Chinese drugs derived from herbs contain minute quantities of substances that could trigger defense mechanisms in our body which strengthen it should not be ignored but, rather, investigated. Western medicine and Chinese medicine have their own individual strong and weak points, and their strong points should be brought together for our benefit. The Chinese have already started the process, and we should emulate them. They know that they have a treasure in their traditional medicine and are working hard to preserve and enrich it.

As I said earlier, the purpose of this book is to present one aspect of Chinese medicine in a practical manner—the way herbs, fruits, and vegetables we are all familiar with are used as Chinese drugs. I have selected 48 well-known specimens. Some of these can be found in the kitchen or garden, while others can be easily bought from supermarkets or neighborhood grocery stores, or from Chinese herb shops or groceries in large cities such as New York, San Francisco, or London. The sources, history, pharmacological effects, and uses of each drug are described in detail. Modern reports of clinical usage, whenever

**Yin,* or "shade," represents the weak, dark, female, negative force, while *yang,* or "sunshine," represents the strong, light, male, positive force. Too much or too little of either produces an imbalance in the body, leading to an illness.

they were available, are also included; most of these have not been reported in English before.

Most of the remedies or recipes given are based on single drugs, while a few contain simple combinations of two or three herbs. Since Chinese herbal remedies as a rule contain multiple drugs, the remedies given in this book are not typical. A few of the remedies are ones that I remember my grandmother giving to us in Hong Kong when we were children—remedies that I remember were helpful in alleviating our conditions. Much of the information on these and other remedies in the book have been drawn from traditional Chinese herbals and technical books in both Chinese and English on botany, chemistry, pharmacology, pharmaceutics, and medicine. A bibliography appears at the end of the book. So also does a glossary of Chinese and other terms that may be unfamiliar to readers in Western countries.

The herbal remedies presented here are, truly, traditional, tested remedies. They have actually been or are still being used by a quarter of the world's population. However, unless otherwise specified, they are not meant to be used on a long-term basis. Throughout this book I have also stressed the lack of quality control in the manufacture of commercial herbal preparations and have tried to discourage the reader from using them. Some remedies may seem farfetched, some quaint, but judgment without a full understanding of the circumstances that surround the use of a drug or remedy is one of the things that has increased the confusion in the West about the value and efficacy of Chinese medicine. I hope this book will enable the reader to take a new look at Chinese medicine, and that, seen as a readily accessible method for a balanced, less drug-dependent life, it will seem less mysterious.

Abbreviations in the text:
cm. centimeters
ft. feet
g. grams
in. inches
kg. kilograms
l. liters
m. meters
mg. milligrams
ml. milliliters
oz. ounces
pt. pints
qt. quarts

ALFALFA AND TOOTHED-BUR CLOVER

苜蓿

General information: Both alfalfa and toothed-bur clover are known in Chinese as *mu xu.* Alfalfa *(Medicago sativa)* is called *zi mu xu,* with *zi,* meaning "purple," referring to the purple color of its flowers. Toothed-bur clover *(Medicago hispida)* is called *nan mu xu,* with *nan* meaning "southern," which probably refers to its origin in southern China.

Both plants belong to the pea family. They are native to Eurasia (especially the Mediterranean region) and have been introduced into America.

Toothed-bur clover is an annual or biennial herb which grows to a height of 1 m. (3.3 ft.) or more and has yellow flowers. It can be found growing in many European countries as well as in waste places throughout the United States and much of Canada, and is cultivated in southern China. In the Western world toothed-bur clover is used primarily as forage.

Alfalfa is a perennial herb of about the same height, with purple flowers. It has a very long taproot that reaches 2 to 5 m. (6–16 ft.) into the ground. Alfalfa grows wild in many parts of the world and is extensively cultivated for forage and other purposes, some of them medicinal. In the United States extracts of alfalfa are used in flavoring beverages and food products. In American folk medicine, the herb is used as a tonic or diuretic, and as a nutrient to increase vitality, appetite, and weight. Interestingly, it is often fed to horses for the same reason. Alfalfa is also said to cure peptic ulcers and other illnesses. It is generally used in teabag, tablet, or capsule form. Alfalfa is also one of the major raw materials for the manufacture of chlorophyll. Alfalfa sprouts are a favorite salad ingredient of many health-conscious Westerners.

Western scientists have done many chemical studies on alfalfa, which contains literally hundreds of biologically active chemicals. Few studies have been reported for toothed-bur clover, but because it is so closely related to alfalfa, we can assume that it has similar constituents. Aside from the usual plant constituents, such as proteins (about 25% based on dry weight), fibers, vitamins, minerals, plant enzymes, and pigments, alfalfa contains 2% to 3% saponin glycosides (which form foams when mixed with water, as soap does), as well as alkaloids, coumarin-type and other compounds.

Due to the fact that alfalfa is made up of such a wide range of chemicals, it is not easy to correlate each of alfalfa's effects on the body with the specific chemical constituents present. However, research has pinpointed some of them. Thus, alfalfa's saponin glycosides are hemolytic (able to break up blood cells), and they can interfere with the utilization of vitamin E by the body. On the other hand, these saponin glycosides have also been shown to lower blood-cholesterol levels in monkeys, thus suggesting their possible benefits as a serum cholesterol-lowering agent for humans.

So far, none of the effects of alfalfa's chemical constituents that has been isolated correlates with the actual uses of *mu xu* in traditional Chinese medicine. But, in light of the fact that alfalfa contains so many chemical constituents whose possible interactions in the human body have not really been explored, it would be foolish to single out one or two of these compounds and try to rationalize their therapeutic role.

Effects on the body: It should be cautioned that some individuals are allergic to alfalfa and may break out with dermatitis, eczema, urticaria (an allergy marked by intense itching), asthma, or rhinitis after drinking alfalfa tea or handling dried alfalfa.

Traditional uses: In Chinese medicine, two parts of alfalfa or boothed-bur clover are used: the aboveground portion (which includes leaves, flowers, and stems) and the root. They are collected from the plant in summer or autumn and are used both fresh and dried.

Although it is not one of the better-known Chinese herbs, and does not have a wide range of uses, *mu xu* (alfalfa or toothed-bur clover) has been used in Chinese medicine at least as far back as the early 6th century A.D. According to the herbals, it is considered bitter-tasting, neutral-natured, and nontoxic. It is believed to cleanse the spleen and stomach, benefit the small and large intestines, and rid the bladder of stones—the purpose for which it is principally used. The usual internal daily dose is 94 to 156 g. (3.3–5.5 oz.) for the fresh herb taken in the form of its expressed juice, or 6 to 9 g. (0.2–0.3 oz.) of the dried herb taken as a powder.

Mu xu root has been used in Chinese medicine at least as far back as the middle of the 7th century A.D. It is considered bitter-tasting and is said to dissipate fever and facilitate urine flow. Major uses of *mu xu* root are in the treatment of jaundice, urinary stones, and night blindness. Specific directions for the use of *mu xu* root in treating urinary stones is described in the *Ben Cao Gang Mu,* as well as in more recent herbals.

It is worth noting that although, according to Western folk medicine, alfalfa is supposed to increase one's appetite and weight, an early 8th-century Chinese herbal for diet therapy states that its prolonged ingestion will "chill" the body and make one lose weight.

Modern uses: The use of fresh southern *mu xu* root (toothed-bur-clover root) in the clinical treatment of night blindness was reported in the *Shansi Journal of Medical and Pharmaceutical Health* in 1960. Four out of six patients with night blindness recovered after being treated with daily doses of 31 g. (1.1 oz.) of a mixture made by cutting the fresh root into small pieces and boiling them in water. The whole mixture (liquid and root) was then taken.

Home remedies: The following examples are quoted from modern herbals.

For treating **bladder stones,** 94 to 156 g. (3.3–5.5 oz.) of fresh southern *mu xu* (toothed-bur clover herb) is pressed to obtain its juice, which is taken internally.

To treat **edema** or **fluid retention,** a soup prepared from 15 g. (0.5 oz.) of powdered dried *mu xu* (alfalfa or toothed-bur-clover) leaves, one piece of bean cake (3–4 oz.), and 94 g. (3.3 oz.) of lard is eaten once daily for several days.

The use of *mu xu* root in treating **jaundice** and **urinary stones** calls for either mashing the fresh herb and then straining the juice through muslin or cheesecloth or boiling the root in water (decoction). When the juice is used, a total daily dose of one jiggerful (1–2 oz.) is taken in two separate portions, after being warmed. For the decoction, a single daily dose of 16 to 31 g. (0.6–1.1 oz.) of the fresh root is used.

Availability: Alfalfa and toothed-bur clover are generally available fresh throughout North America and Europe in the form of weeds. Powdered alfalfa in capsules is available from health food stores, but you can never be sure whether it is really alfalfa when it is in powder form. *Mu xu* (alfalfa or toothed-bur clover) is also available as a dried herb from some Chinese herb shops.

ALMOND

杏仁

General Information: Both sweet and bitter almonds are obtained from the almond tree, which is known botanically as *Prunus amygdalus* of the rose family. The almond tree is native to western Asia and is now extensively cultivated in the Mediterranean countries, western Asia, South Africa, South Australia, California, and northwestern China. It has several varieties, two of which, var. *dulcis* and *amara,* yield sweet and bitter almonds respectively. The fruit of the almond tree is technically the same as a peach or apricot except that its outer portion is leathery, not fleshy and edible like the peach; the seed inside its hard stony pit yields the almond. In Western countries, the word "almonds" (sweet and bitter) refers strictly to seeds of the almond tree. In China, the term "almonds" refers not only to Western almonds but also to apricot pits. The latter are actually more commonly used. In Chinese medicine, apricot kernel is known as *xing ren* and the Western almond as *ba dan xing ren,* with *ba dan* denoting its foreign origin.

Sweet almonds are used as food in Western countries, but bitter almonds are not. In the United States, sweet almonds are generally referred to simply as almonds. Since bitter almonds are considered poisonous and usually are not available to consumers, there appears to be little need for differentiation.

In China and in Chinese communities overseas, sweet almonds and bitter almonds are both readily available, the latter usually in herb stores. Although the Chinese also consider bitter almonds poisonous, they nevertheless use them quite frequently as medicine as well as for food. Sweet almonds used by the Chinese are derived from the sweet varieties of the almond tree as well as the apricot tree *(Prunus armeniaca),* while bitter almonds are derived from their bitter varieties. The bitter-apricot kernel or bitter Western almond is also called *bei xing* (northern almond) while the sweet variety is called *nan xing* (southern almond), probably in reference to their respective commercial sources in China. The apricot is a native of China but is now grown in many parts of the world, especially in California, North Africa, Japan, and northern China.

The most important difference between sweet and bitter almonds is the amount of amygdalin they contain. Amygdalin is a chemical compound containing cyanide which when broken down by enzymes produces the deadly hydrocyanic acid. It also yields glucose and benzaldehyde. The latter is a chemical that has the characteristic "almond" (more correctly, bitter-almond) aroma. Bitter almonds, as well as apricot pits from the bitter variety of apricot, contain 3% to 4% of amygdalin, while sweet almonds (including the pits from sweet apricots) contain little or no amygdalin.

Both sweet and bitter almonds contain large amounts of oil (35%–55%) and protein (18%–25%), as well as important minerals (potassium, calcium, phosphorus, copper, zinc, etc.) and vitamins (especially B vitamins). Hence, when used as a food, sweet almonds are quite nutritious.

Two commercial products are derived from almonds—sweet-almond oil (also known simply as almond oil) and bitter-almond oil.

Sweet-almond oil is prepared from both bitter and sweet almonds by pressing the kernels. This oil contains neither hydrocyanic acid nor benzaldehyde, hence it is not toxic and has no almond aroma. It is soothing to the skin and has mildly laxative properties. For these reasons, it is used as an ingredient in cosmetic and pharmaceutic creams, lotions, ointments, and soaps to prevent chapping, and as a laxative in doses up to 30 ml. (1 fl. oz.). It is also used as a lubricant for delicate mechanisms such as watches and firearms.

Bitter-almond oil is prepared from bitter almonds or other kernels that contain sizable quantities of amygdalin, such as apricot, peach, and plum kernels. The kernels (e.g., bitter almonds) used have usually already been pressed to obtain any nonvolatile oil, such as sweet-almond oil. To prepare bitter-almond oil, the cake form that remains is soaked in lukewarm water for 12 to 24 hours. During this soaking process the enzymes in the cake break amygdalin down to glucose, benzaldehyde, and hydrocyanic acid. The mixture is subsequently distilled by passing steam through it; benzaldehyde and hydrocyanic acid are carried out by the steam and collected as bitter-almond oil. This oil contains over 95% benzaldehyde and 2% to 4% hydrocyanic acid. Up to 1960 it was an officially recognized drug in the United

States and was used in cough remedies as well as locally to relieve itching. However, it is no longer used.

After the removal of the deadly hydrocyanic acid, the resulting bitter-almond oil is practically pure benzaldehyde, and is usually called "bitter-almond oil, FFPA" (FFPA meaning free from prussic acid, an outdated term for hydrocyanic acid). This oil is extensively used to flavor various food products and beverages such as liqueurs.

Effects on the body: Bitter-almond oil, FFPA has local anesthetic and muscle-relaxant properties. Although free from hydrocyanic acid, 50 to 60 ml. (1.7–2 oz.) of it taken internally can be fatal, due to the toxic effects of benzaldehyde, which causes a slowdown of the central nervous system and respiratory failure.

Traditional uses: Almonds have been used in Western countries for several thousand years—one foodstuff that has had a longer history here than in China. They were known in Biblical times, and are mentioned in the Old Testament. Although Western almonds probably were not introduced into the practice of Chinese medicine until a few centuries ago, their Chinese counterparts, the apricot kernels, have a long history of use. The first recorded use of the apricot kernel in Chinese medicine dates back to the Han Dynasty (206 B.C. to A.D. 220). The Shennong Herbal lists it in the toxic-drug category. It has since been described in most major Chinese herbals, including the *Ben Cao Gang Mu,* and is currently an official drug in the pharmacopeia of the People's Republic of China.

As I noted, although both bitter and sweet varieties of almond are used in chinese medicine, the bitter variety is more commonly used as medicine while the sweet variety is more commonly used as food. The northern almond (bitter almond) is acrid-tasting and is considered toxic. It is said to have warming properties, and to act on the lungs and large intestine, break up phlegm, stop coughs, control wheezing, and lubricate the intestines. The southern almond (sweet almond) is pleasant-tasting and is considered to be neutral and non-toxic in nature. Its uses are similar to those of the northern almond.

Although the sweet almond and the sweet-apricot kernel and the bitter almond and the bitter-apricot kernel are used to treat similar illnesses, most recorded uses refer to the bitter varieties.

The best-known traditional uses of the almond and apricot kernel are in the treatment of coughs, excessive phlegm, asthma, and constipation. Daily internal doses range from 4.5 to 9 g. (0.2–0.3 oz.). When mashed, the kernels are also used externally to treat skin sores, toothache, dog bites, and snakebites.

Since apricot kernels have been used extensively by the Chinese over a number of centuries, incidences of apricot-kernel poisoning were inevitable. Bitter-almond or apricot-kernel poisoning produces symptoms that include dizziness, fainting, nausea, vomiting, headache, convulsions, irregular breathing, and coma, among others. To treat this type of poisoning, traditional Chinese medicine has made use of the root and bark of the apricot tree, and recent Chinese medical reports have documented successful treatments. Eighty poisoned patients were each fed a filtered decoction of the bark prepared by boiling 62 g. (2.2 oz.) of bark in 500 ml. (17 fl. oz.) of water for 20 minutes. All recovered. They generally showed signs of recovery —regaining consciousness, with breathing returning to normal and nausea and vomiting disappearing—two hours after being fed the mixture. And recovery was complete four hours after the treatment was started. As with most traditional Chinese remedies, it is not known exactly how this remedy works. The active ingredients of the bark or root are also not really understood. However, it certainly appears to be simpler and cheaper to treat bitter-almond (cyanide) poisoning this way than to use the modern Western method of injecting the patient with numerous drugs, inserting tubes into his lungs and stomach, washing out his stomach, and applying artificial respiration.

Modern uses: More recently, sweet- and bitter-apricot kernels have been used, mashed or as an oil paste, in the treatment of vulvar pruritus (itching of the female external genitals) and vaginal trichomoniasis (discharge caused by a parasite), as well as internally in the treatment of chronic bronchitis. Their effectiveness has been documented in several Chinese clinical reports during the past two decades.

Home remedies: During dry weather conditions, to soothe the lungs and to treat or prevent **dry throat** and **dry cough,** the Chinese in Hong Kong and southern China, especially the Cantonese, use "almond tea" or "almond milk," a very popular drink prepared from apricot kernels. To prepare the drink, 10 parts sweet almonds and one part bitter almonds are soaked in water, together with a small amount of rice. After the almonds and rice are well soaked and become tender, they are ground to a paste, usually in a small granite mill which many Chinese families have. The resulting milky mixture is strained to remove the coarse particles, and then diluted with water and cooked with sugar or, more commonly, rock candy to taste. The finished almond tea has a consistency ranging from thin to relatively thick, depending on the amount of water or rice used. It was one of my favorite drinks when I was growing up in Hong Kong.

Availability: Sweet almonds are widely available in groceries and supermarkets, while bitter almonds are available only in medicinal form from Chinese herb shops.

ALOE VERA

芦荟

General Information: Known in Chinese as *lu hui,* aloe vera has become a household term in the West during the past few years. The aloe-vera plant, a species of the lily family, is now sold at many florists, garden centers, and health food stores in major cities in the United States and in some other Western countries. The plant acquires different characteristics depending on whether it is grown indoors or outdoors. Since it cannot survive freezing temperatures, it is cultivated only in regions with warm climates, such as the southern states of Texas, Florida, and Arizona, and the Caribbean islands (Bonaire, Barbados, Aruba, etc.). The aloe-vera plant is a succulent perennial.

It has hardly any stem when young but develops a short stem as it matures. In an outdoor environment, the plant reaches a height of 0.6 to 1 m. (2–3 ft.) in three to five years. A typical mature leaf at this stage is 45 to 60 cm. (1.5–2 ft.) long, 7.5 to 10 cm. (3–4 in.) across at the base, and 1.5 to 2.5 cm. (0.7–1.1 in.) thick. When it flowers, it produces a flowering stalk that can reach as high as 1.2 m. (4 ft.) above the ground. A mature plant also produces numerous sucker plants (commonly called "babies") at its base, which are usually about 10 to 15 cm. (4–6 in.) tall. These are used to plant new fields or are potted and sold through florists and garden centers as "household" aloe vera. This household plant is what most Americans know. When grown indoors, it seldom attains more than half the size of its outdoor counterpart and almost never produces flowers. In fact, aloe-vera plants grown in American households generally are only 15 to 20 cm. (6–8 in.) tall, with their larger leaves measuring 15 to 25 cm. (6–10 in.) long and 2 to 3.5 cm. (0.8–1.5 in.) wide at their base. Most leaves of the indoor plant are dotted with white spots, whereas only very young leaves of the outdoor plant are spotted.

Currently two major commercial products (drug aloe and aloe-vera gel) are obtained from the leaves of aloe-vera plants. Drug aloe is derived from the bitter yellow juice that is drained from the base of the leaves after they are cut. This juice is present in specialized cells immediately beneath the thick skin (epidermis) of the aloe leaf. Aloe-vera gel is derived from the mucilaginous gel present in the middle portion of the leaf beneath the cells that produce the yellow juice.

Drug aloe and aloe-vera gel are two completely different products, and one should not be confused with the other.

Drug aloe is produced mainly in South Africa and in the Caribbean countries. Besides *Aloe vera,* which is also known as *Aloe barbadensis,* other *Aloe* species are also used. In China, a domestic variety called *Aloe vera* var. *chinensis* is used. To produce the drug, the leaves are cut at their base and the bitter yellow juice is allowed to drain out completely into a copper or other suitable vessel (e.g., a gasoline or petrol can) and heat-dried. This crude drug aloe comes in the form of irregular reddish-brown to dark-brown masses. It is a well-known purgative, containing anthraglycosides as its active principles, and is listed as a purgative drug in the pharmacopeias of Great Britain, Switzerland, Germany, France, the United States, and the People's Republic of China, although in the United States it is officially recognized only for external use. Drug aloe is found in many over-the-counter laxative preparations sold in the United States and Europe, and is also used in certain diet drugs and in cosmetics. When drug aloe is used in cosmetics, the products are often marketed to imply that aloe-vera gel has been used, and the consumer has no way of telling from the label which is actually present.

Aloe-vera gel, commonly known simply as "aloe vera," is produced mainly in the United States, where it has become big business, with retail sales of over $1 billion in 1982. It is being promoted by some companies as a cure-all. In one promotion brochure, aloe vera is recommended for 88 illnesses. The fresh gel of aloe vera is well known for its effectiveness in treating minor skin burns, sunburn, and other minor wounds and skin irritations, although the properties responsible are still unknown. It also moisturizes and softens the skin and promotes the healing of surface wounds without scars. For this reason, it is also known as the "burn," "first-aid," or "medicine" plant in American folk medicine. Other uses for aloe-vera gel in Western folk medicine include the treatment of ringworm, venereal sores, boils, eczema, hemorrhoids, chronic conjunctivitis, baldness, tumors, colds, dysentery, kidney pains, coughs, and insect bites.

Aloe vera is used both externally and internally. Due to the astronomical growth of the industry during the past few years with a large number of companies trying to cash in on aloe vera's mystique, a large number of food, drug, and cosmetic products in the United States claim aloe vera as their major constituent. Although some of the companies and promoters make claims about the effectiveness or purity of their aloe-vera products (some based on so-called patented processes, others on secret company formulas), the fact is that none of these claims has been proven, either scientifically, through unbiased research, or empirically, after generations of use. Furthermore, there is still no scientific test to distinguish a product that contains genuine aloe vera from one that contains no aloe vera or contains only adulterants such as vegetable gums or water. Similarly, there is no way to prove claims that the products are, as they are often declared, "purified," "stabilized," "pure," or "natural." The only sure way to obtain genuine aloe-vera gel is to use a fresh leaf of the aloe-vera plant. With so much freedom and so few restrictions on manufacture, it is easy to imagine how the industry could grow from less than $100 million dollars in 1976 to $1 billion in 1982.

Although, since it has become commercially glamorous, the claims made about aloe vera have become excessive, they are nevertheless based on medicinal and cosmetic properties of the original aloe-vera plant that have been long recognized.

Traditional uses: Aloe vera has been used in medicine in Western countries for several thousand years. Early Greeks and Egyptians, for example, seem to have used drug aloe primarily, but Cleopatra's beauty is believed to have been enhanced by her use of the gel.

The first recorded use of drug aloe in Chinese medicine dates back to the beginning of the Tang Dynasty, in the early part of the 7th century A.D., but it was probably introduced much earlier. According to the herbals, drug aloe is bitter-tasting and considered to be cold-natured (capable of reducing fever or heat), acting on the liver, spleen, stomach, and large intestine to dissipate fever, promote bowel movement, and kill parasites. It is traditionally used to treat constipation, amenorrhea (absence of menses), convulsions in children, internal worms, ringworm, and atrophic rhinitis (inflammation of the mucous membrane of the nose). Drug aloe is mainly taken internally, in the form of pills or powders. In ringworm treatment, a powdered form is applied directly on the affected area.

Although the actions of drug aloe are rather strong, Chinese medicine generally considers it nontoxic. In fact, a popular traditional remedy for constipation, called *geng yi wan* (bathroom pills), which dates back to the early part of the 19th century, is composed of 41% drug aloe, 30% cinnabar, and 29% starch, and cinnabar is a commonly used Chinese drug that contains mostly mercury and *is* considered toxic. However, remedies like this that are still being used are clearly relatively safe or they would have been discarded by now.

Compared to drug aloe, the history of the use of aloe-vera gel in Chinese medicine is relatively short—only two to three hundred years. Both *Aloe vera* and its Chinese variety, *Aloe vera* var. *chinensis,* are used. They are both cultivated in southern China, but the latter is much more common. The major uses of the fresh gel are for burns, sores, abscesses, hematuria (bloody urine), coughing blood, whooping cough, calluses, and leukorrhea (white vaginal discharge). But the gel itself isn't often used. Instead, usually, the whole leaf is mashed, or the juice and gel are both pressed out of the leaf and then used. The resulting medicine contains not only the gel but also the drug aloe that is present in the bitter juice. And because of the laxative properties of drug aloe, fresh aloe leaf is also used for treating constipation.

Modern uses: Whereas in most Western pharmacopeias the only officially recognized use of drug aloe is in treating constipation, in the pharmacopeia of the People's Republic of China its use in treating internal worms, convulsions, and ringworm is also officially sanctioned. But in both the Chinese and Western pharmacopeias, pregnant women are warned against using drug aloe, since it may cause abortion.

The fresh aloe leaf is also used to prevent radiation burns. A remedy published in 1971 by the Institute of Nuclear Medicine of the Chinese Academy of Medical Sciences (similar to the U.S. National Academy of Science) calls for blending 30 ml. (about 1 fl. oz.) of liquid from the freshly mashed leaf, 20 g. (0.7 oz.) of gum arabic, 0.5 ml. of eucalyptus oil as a preservative, and sufficient castor oil to make up 100 ml. (about 3 oz.) of the mixture. The resulting emulsion is painted on areas of the skin to be exposed to radiation and allowed to dry.

During the past five decades, numerous scientific studies have been published on the effectiveness of aloe-vera gel in treating radiation and thermal burns, wounds, chapped and dry skin, peptic ulcers, leg ulcers, and skin conditions. Although these findings have not been conclusive, they do offer substantiation for some of the traditional uses of aloe-vera gel.

Home remedies: Most remedies calling for aloe are quite complicated and combine numerous other herbs. But a simple one for **constipation** is given below. About 15 g. (0.5 oz.) of fresh leaf with skin is boiled with two cups of water until it is down to about one-half cup. The liquid is strained off or decanted, and the resulting bitter liquid is taken before retiring for the night.

Availability: Drug aloe in its crude form is available in herb shops and Chinese herb stores in major Western cities. As noted, the aloe-vera plant is available in most garden centers and in some flower shops and supermarkets in major cities. Mature aloe-vera leaves are also now available in some health food stores.

BANANA (Plantain)

香蕉

General information: Bananas are the fruits of *Musa paradisiaca* var. *sapientum* of the banana family. The plant is a tropical perennial herb native to tropical Asia. Although 3 to 9 m. (10–30 ft.) tall, it is regarded botanically as an herb because of its nonwoody nature. Its stem is not a real stem in the usual sense of the word, but rather a false stem formed by the bases of its leaves wrapped tightly together. Its leaf blades are 1.5 to 3 m. (5–10 ft.) long and 40 to 60 cm. (1.3–2 ft.) broad. Bananas are now produced commercially in most tropical regions of the world, including southern China, Taiwan, the Philippines, Indonesia, and Thailand in the Far East, Ivory Coast, Cameroon, and Somalia in Africa, and tropical American countries such as Costa Rica, Honduras, Brazil, Colombia, and Ecuador.

There are many types of bananas. Although their flavors and tastes are similar, there are subtle differences, depending on the varieties and where they are produced. Bananas are now a favorite food both in the East and in the West. They are generally eaten raw after removing the peel. Occasionally they are eaten after having been dried or cooked.

Plantains, close relatives of the banana, are the fruit of *Musa paradisiaca.* Also known as "cooking bananas," they are rather popular among Latin Americans and Chinese and are the chief staple food in parts of East Africa. Latin Americans—Colombians, for example—usually eat plantains cooked, while Chinese generally eat them raw. Plantains taste different from bananas; they are less fragrant but more mucilaginous, or sticky.

Bananas are known in Chinese as *xiang jiao,* meaning "fragrant banana," and plantains are known as *da jiao,* meaning "big banana" (the "big" probably referring to the usually larger diameter). Pound for pound, plantain contains more calories than banana. According to recent figures published by the U.S. Department of Agriculture, raw plantain contains about 31% carbohydrates but raw banana contains only about 22%. Both contain about 1% protein and about 0.38% potassium. Although banana has been widely recommended as a rich source of potassium, its actual potassium content is not very much higher than in other common fruits. Avocado, numerous types of beans (such as soybean and lima bean), peanuts, almonds, walnuts, and other nuts are much richer in potassium. Even commercial orange juice contains over half the potassium (about 0.2%) found in banana. Thus, drinking two glasses of orange juice would provide you with as much potassium as eating two or three bananas. It is possible that Western physicians have been recommending banana inadvertently for its other nutritional or therapeutic properties rather than for its potassium content.

Effects on the body: Plantain and banana have been shown to contain two human hormones, noradrenaline and serotonin, and to have antibacterial properties.

In Western culture, banana is generally considered to be a neutralizer. It is used for both diarrhea and constipation and is sometimes recommended by pediatricians for these conditions in infants. Banana is also considered a food that is especially good for children.

Traditional uses: Although both banana and plantain are used in Chinese medicine, plantain is generally considered to have been the original drug, while banana was introduced more recently. The first recorded use of plantain in Chinese medicine dates back to the 7th century A.D. It is considered pleasant- or sweet-tasting and cold-natured. It is said to dissipate fever, lubricate the intestines, and rid the body of poisons. According to the folk medicine of Guangdong, one of the provinces of China where plantain originated, there are some differences between plantain and banana in their therapeutic, and what are possibly toxic, properties. The Cantonese regard raw plantain as harmless and believe it can be ingested for long periods of time even by ill and weak persons. Raw banana, however, is not recommended for long-term ingestion, especially not for weak persons or persons with illnesses such as asthma and other lung conditions.

Major traditional uses of plantain and banana include the treatment of constipation, diarrhea, and bleeding due to hemorrhoids.

The sun-dried peel of plantain or banana (known in Chinese as *da jiao pi*) is also used in Cantonese folk medicine. Taken internally, in the form of a decoction, it is used to treat dysentery and abdominal pain caused by cholera. Applied externally, the decoction is used to treat skin itching due to flea and other insect bites.

The first recorded medicinal use of the rootstock of the plantain plant *(gan jiao gen)* predates that of plantain itself; it dates back to the 6th century A.D. The rootstock is considered pleasant or sweet, yet astringent-tasting and cold-natured. In the form of its expressed juice, it is either taken internally or applied externally to treat skin abscesses and sores.

Modern uses: The clinical use of the fresh juice of plantain rootstock in treating epidemic B-type encephalitis was reported in two southern Chinese public health journals in 1970 and 1972. Of 117 patients treated with daily oral doses of 1,000 to 1,500 ml. (33–50 oz.), 110 recovered, one still had residual symptoms after treatment, and six died. In most cases, patients' body temperatures started to return to normal three to four days after treatment began. Encephalitis B is a viral disease, and it appears that plantain rootstock possesses antiviral properties.

Home remedies: For treating **hemorrhoids** and bleeding due to hemorrhoids, one remedy, in a well-known herbal from southern China, calls for stewing two unpeeled plantains or bananas and eating both, peel and all.

Availability: Bananas are widely available, especially at fruit stands, groceries, and supermarkets. Plantains are available in health food stores, ethnic (especially Latin American) groceries, and specialty sections of some supermarkets.

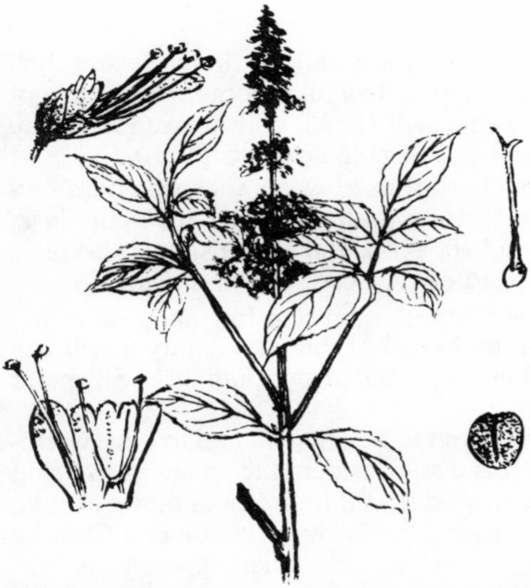

BASIL

罗勒

General information: Also known as sweet basil and common basil, basil is a common spice or herb used by many peoples around the world. It is known in Chinese as *luo le,* and botanically as *Ocimum basilicum* of the mint family. Basil is a fragrant, hairy, annual herb, which grows to a height of about 70 cm. (2.3 ft.). There are many varieties, with different chemical compositions and flavor characteristics. It is native to Africa and tropical Asia but is now cultivated worldwide.

Basil's dried leaves and flowering tops constitute the well-known spice which is used domestically and in Chartreuse liqueur. The whole aboveground herb is used in Western folk medicine. In Chinese medicine, the whole dried herb is normally used, but so are individual parts, such as the roots and fruits (seeds). The herb is normally collected early in autumn. After it is cleaned of dirt and sand it is cut into short sections and dried under the sun or in the shade. The basil seeds are also collected and sun-dried at this time. They are cleaned by sifting, since washing them with water makes them clump together when dry.

Basil contains a small amount of volatile oil which is composed of many aroma or fragrance chemicals, including linalool, estragole, eugenol, borneol, ocimene, and geraniol. The relative proportions of these chemicals vary considerably depending on the variety of basil. According to U.S. Department of Agriculture figures, basil also contains 14% protein, 61% carbohydrates, 4% fats, minerals (especially potassium and calcium, at 3.4% and 2.1% respectively), and vitamins (especially A and C).

Basil seeds contain 17% fats (in the form of oil), 16% protein, 28%

fibers, and 23% carbohydrates, including various simple sugars such as glucose, mannose, and arabinose. The oil is composed mainly of linoleic acid (56%) and linolenic acid (19%), both unsaturated fatty acids; oleic acid is also present in sizable amounts (15%).

In Western folk medicine, basil is used as an antispasmodic, carminative, and stomachic in treating gastrointestinal problems (e.g., stomach cramps, vomiting, constipation, and enteritis). It is also used to treat whooping cough, head colds, headache, and warts.

Traditional uses: Used in Chinese medicine for many centuries, basil was first mentioned in an herbal of the 6th century A.D. It has since been described in other major herbals, including Li Shizhen's *Ben Cao Gang Mu.*

Traditionally, basil is considered to be pungent and to have warming (invigorating) qualities. It is also considered to range from being nontoxic to being slightly toxic and is said to promote blood circulation, to help digestion, and to rid the body of conditions Chinese medicine considers to be toxic, such as inflammation, swellings, and sores.

Various other conditions also treated with basil include headache resulting from colds, stomachache, indigestion, diarrhea, irregular menstruation, skin sores, itching from hives, traumatic injuries, and snake and insect bites. When used internally, the usual daily dose is 6 to 12 g. (0.2–0.4 oz.) boiled in water. For external use, mashed fresh basil is applied directly, or a decoction is used for washing the affected areas. Another method is to apply powdered, burnt basil (ash) directly.

In traditional Chinese medicine, basil seeds are used mainly for treating bloodshot eyes that secrete excessively, cloudy cornea (nebula), ingrown eyelashes, and other eye problems. They are also used to treat tooth-socket problems (e.g., pyorrhea). The usual internal daily dose is 2.5 to 4.7 g. (0.1–0.2 oz.) taken as a decoction.

Home remedies: Several remedies using basil herb or basil seeds are recorded in classical herbals, but most of them are complicated mixtures of herbs. The following are two of the simpler ones.

To treat **cough,** an 8th-century recipe calls for eating bread prepared with 62 g. (2.2 oz.) fresh basil leaves, 125 g. (4.4 oz.) fresh ginger, 3 g. (0.1 oz.) white pepper, 125 g. (4.4 oz.) flour, and a small amount of salt. After cooking, the bread is eaten on an empty stomach.

To treat **cloudy cornea,** seven basil seeds are boiled slowly in water. The resulting decoction is drunk before going to bed at night. It is said to be effective with long-term use.

Availability: Basil leaves are readily available in grocery stores and supermarkets. The herb and seeds can be bought in some Chinese herb shops. Basil can also be grown easily in home gardens.

BEAN CURD

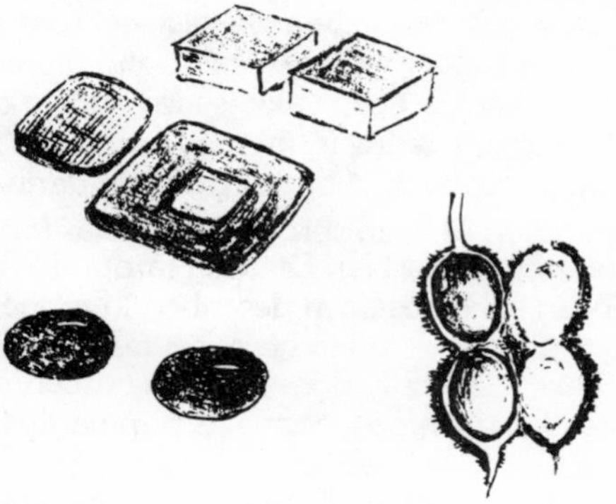

豆腐

General information: Bean curd is also called tofu and bean cake and in Chinese is known as *dou fu.* It is a very important source of protein and calcium or magnesium in the Chinese diet. Since most Chinese do not drink milk or eat much meat, regular ingestion of bean curd and related products probably has kept them from calcium, magnesium, and protein deficiency problems throughout their existence.

In recent years, due to the fact that Westerners have become increasingly health conscious and, as a result, have started to eat less meat and demand more protein products made from vegetable sources, bean curd is now available in many major cities in the Western world.

Although bean cake is made primarily from soybean, other beans, such as mung bean, may also be used. The beans (commonly the yellow variety of soybean) are soaked in water for about 24 hours until they are well swollen, then ground into a thin paste with water (at home an electric blender can be used). The ground mixture is then strained through a piece of clean cloth, and a residue (known as bean-curd residue) and a liquid are obtained. The liquid, after boiling, is known as soybean milk. When this soybean milk is treated with a small amount of a solution of gypsum (calcium sulfate) or, occasionally, of magnesium salts such as Epsom salts, a curd is formed. Part of the water is removed from the curd by pressing it between layers of cloth or muslin. The resulting bean curd contains about 85% water and 8% protein; one pound of it yields about 300 calories. This is the type commonly known to Westerners; it is usually sold packed in water. And, unless otherwise specified, this is the type to which I shall refer when discussing medicinal uses. Although to most Westerners bean curd is bean curd, in fact there are various types, including dried bean cake, fried bean cake, and fermented bean cake—all derived from bean curd. Most Chinese vegetarian fake-meat dishes are prepared from bean cake, dried bean cake, fried bean cake, and gluten. Because of its offensive odor, fermented bean cake is also known as "Chinese cheese." As with Limburger cheese, fermented bean cake is unpalatable unless one is brought up with it or is extremely daring.

Traditional uses: The preparation of bean curd and its use as food and in Chinese medicine date back to the Han Dynasty (around 200 B.C.). Through the centuries bean cake has been described in numerous classical Chinese herbals. It is considered to be sweet-tasting and to have cooling properties. Since it actually does not have much of a taste, it can be made to taste like anything—hence its popularity in vegetarian dishes.

Bean-cake residue has been used medicinally mainly for skin conditions such as ulcers and sores, for which both the uncooked and cooked (baked) forms are made into patties and applied directly onto the affected skin. According to an old traditional remedy, fried bean-cake residue taken with a cup of tea is said to heal bloody feces due to intestinal bleeding.

Home remedies: Although bean curd has been used as a traditional Chinese drug, it does not seem to have any specific medicinal properties. Descriptions of its usage in Chinese herbals are rather general and vague; usually it is mentioned as one of numerous ingredients in a remedy. Nevertheless, a remedy from an early 16th-century herbal using bean curd alone for treating **alcohol intoxication** may be of interest. This remedy was for a person "so drunk that the whole body is red and purple like dead except with head and heart still warm." For this condition, hot bean curd (the temperature is not specified) is cut into slices and repeatedly applied all over the body until the patient revives. This is a rather unusual application, and I have no idea how useful it is. However, one should not dismiss it outright without more information. Remember that acupuncture, once considered "poking needles in one's body" in the West, is slowly being accepted.

The most common use of bean cake, at least in southern China from which my family came, is in treating the **common cold.** It seems that every Cantonese grandmother knows about it, and mine was no exception. When I was a child I had my share of colds, for which I took my share of "bean-cake tea," a well-known cold remedy which is actually more of a soup. It is probably called "tea" to differentiate it from bean-cake soups—soups that contain bean cake and have nothing to do with the cold remedy.

The essential ingredients for bean-cake tea are bean cake and green onions; optional ingredients include fresh mint leaves, ginger, and fermented black beans. My grandmother used bean cake, green onions, and fermented black beans. To prepare this "tea," 6–8 oz. of bean cake is lightly browned in a small amount of vegetable oil; two or three whole green onions and a small amount (1–2 teaspoons) of fermented black beans are added, followed by two cups of water. The liquid is cooked down to about one cup, and the whole mixture is eaten while still hot. This remedy used to work for me, stopping or greatly slowing down my runny nose by the next day, and my cold symptoms would disappear on the third or fourth day. Of course, most common colds last one to a few days without medical attention; the duration depends on one's physical condition and whether or not one has enough rest. It is possible that bean-cake tea supplies the body with necessary nutrients to help fight the cold. Nobody knows. But one must remember that the practice of Chinese medicine is based on the principle of balancing the different functions of the body (thus strengthening it) to prevent or cure illnesses.

Availability: Bean curd is available in Chinese groceries, health food stores, and sometimes in supermarkets.

CASSIA

肉桂

General information: Cassia, or Chinese cinnamon, is generally regarded as different from the common Saigon or Ceylon cinnamon on your kitchen shelf, which the food industry prefers for use in food products because of its better flavor. However, pharmaceutical manufacturers use cassia and the other types of cinnamon interchangeably. For the average nontechnical person, the difference in flavor is too minor to be noticeable.

Cassia is the dried bark of the stem or branches of *Cinnamomum cassia* of the laurel family, a tree that can reach a height of 12 to 17 m. (36–51 ft.). For cassia production the trees are usually cultivated and coppiced (cut back) so that they do not grow too tall for easy harvesting. There are various types of cassia, but the two most common are quills and strips. The former are obtained from young trees (five to six years old); the latter, from old trees. Cassia is produced only in China, where it is called *rou gui.* Guangxi, Guangdong, and Yunnan are the major producing provinces. A sizable amount goes into the production of cassia oil (Chinese cinnamon oil), which, like regular cinnamon oil, is extensively used in the West for flavoring food and pharmaceutical products.

Cassia contains 1% to 2% volatile oil (cassia oil), which is mainly responsible for the spicy aroma and taste. Like other bark materials, it also contains tannins, sugars, resins, and mucilage, among other constituents. The volatile oil contains many chemicals used in the manufacture of fragrances or flavorings. Cinnamaldehyde, the one present in the highest amount (75%–90%) has been demonstrated in scientific experiments to have sedative and pain-relieving effects on mice.

Both cassia and standard cinnamon have been used for thousands of years in both Eastern and Western cultures in treating chronic diarrhea, rheumatism, colds, high blood pressure, kidney conditions, and abdominal pain.

Effects on the body: Chinese and Japanese scientists have found that cassia has sedative effects and lowers high blood pressure and fever in experimental animals. The oil has antiseptic properties, killing various types of bacteria and fungi.

Traditional uses: Cassia has been used medicinally in China for several thousand years. Its first recorded use dates back to the Han Dynasty (200 B.C.–A.D. 200), when it was described in the Shennong Herbal under the nontoxic category of herbs. It is now considered slightly toxic and to have warming effects. When relatively large amounts (1.3 oz. and over) are ingested, toxic symptoms include dizziness, blurred vision, cough, dry thirst, and decreased urine flow. These are considered to be "hot" conditions and generally require cooling herbs such as mung beans or chrysanthemum flowers for their treatment.

Traditionally, Chinese cinnamon is used to treat coid hands and feet, weak pulse, headache, lumbago, aching knees, wheezing, shortness of breath, menstrual pain, amenorrhea (abnormal menstrual periods), and abdominal pain with vomiting. The usual daily dose is 1 to 4.5 g. (0.04–0.16 oz.) taken as a powder or as a decoction or tea.

Cassia oil is used mainly as a carminative (for relieving colic and griping) or as a stomach tonic. The usual daily dose is 0.06 to 0.6 ml. (1–10 drops) taken with water.

Home remedies: Of the many recorded remedies, most use cassia in combination with numerous other herbs. The following are two of the simpler ones.

For treating **bellyache** and **diarrhea** resulting from **stomach and intestinal upsets,** cassia powder and clove powder are mixed evenly in equal amounts (28 g. or 1 oz. each), and the mixture is taken either internally or applied externally. For internal use, the powder is swallowed with water; the daily dose is 0.6 to 1.6 g. (0.02–0.06 oz.). For external application, a small amount of the powder is spread evenly on an adhesive tape about 6 cm. by 6 cm. (2.5 in. by 2.5 in.) which is then taped over the navel area.

To treat **traumatic injuries** (e.g., from fist fights, bumps, or falls) resulting in **blood congestion** and an **aching body,** about 6 g. (0.2 oz.) of powdered cassia is taken with wine.

Availability: Cassia is sold in health food stores and in Chinese herb shops.

CHRYSANTHEMUM

菊花

General information: Both wild and cultivated chrysanthemums are used in Chinese medicine.

Wild chrysanthemum *(ye ju),* as the name implies, grows wild in China, and the flowers are gathered from meadows, woods, hills, and roadsides. It is known botanically as *Chrysanthemum indicum* of the composite family. Although its uses are similar to those of the cultivated chrysanthemum, it is much less commonly used.

The origin of the cultivated chrysanthemum is unclear. It is believed to be a descendant of the wild chrysanthemum or of *Chrysanthemum morifolium* (which also originated in Asia), depending on which authority one consults. The plant is a perennial, 0.5 to 1.4 m. (1.5–4.6 ft.) tall. In the Western world, it is commonly known as florists' chrysanthemum, and has many varieties. For medicinal use, the flower heads are gathered in late autumn when they are fully opened. They are either sun-dried, dried in the shade, oven-dried, or first steamed and then sun-dried. The drying process is laborious and time-consuming. For example, drying in the shade may take weeks to complete. The dried flowers, called chrysanthemum flowers, are known in Chinese as *ju hua.* They range in size from 1 to 2 cm. (0.4–0.8 in.) across and are off-white or yellowish in color.

Effects on the body: Although practically no Western scientific research, other than limited chemical studies, has been done on chrysanthemum flowers, the abilities of this drug to fight inflammations (e.g., conjunctivitis), high blood pressure, and skin diseases have been well known in China for centuries. During the past few decades, many of the medicinal properties of chrysanthemum flowers, including their antibacterial and antiviral effects, have been reported in Chinese and Japanese scientific journals, including regional and national journals of microbiology, medicine, and pharmaceutics.

Some individuals are allergic to chrysanthemum flowers or leaves and develop dermatitis from contact. These individuals should stay away from chrysanthemums or their related plants.

Traditional uses: Chrysanthemum flowers have been used in Chinese medicine for several thousand years. This drug was listed in the Shennong Herbal under the nontoxic category. It has a pleasant yet bitter taste and is considered to have cooling properties. It is said to improve one's vision, lower fever, drive away external disease-causing factors (e.g., allergies and microbes), and detoxify the body. Major traditional uses of chrysanthemum flowers include treatment of headache, dizziness, redness of the eyes, excessive tearing, boils, sores, and abscesses.

Modern uses: As I said earlier, there have been a number of relatively recent studies in China and Japan of the medicinal effects of chrysanthemum flowers. For example, a 1972 report in a Chinese national pharmaceutical journal described the clinical use of chrysanthemum tea in treating high blood pressure and its associated symptoms such as headache, dizziness, and insomnia. A mixture of 25 to 31 g. (about 1 oz.) each of chrysanthemum flowers and honeysuckle was divided into four portions. Boiling water was added to one portion and allowed to steep for 10 to 15 minutes, and the resulting tea was taken. A second steeping of the flower heads was made and the tea was also drunk. The same procedure was followed three more times that day. All four portions of the mixture were used each day for up to 30 days. Of 46 patients thus treated, 35 showed improvement in their symptoms, with blood pressure returning to normal in three to seven days. The remaining patients also showed varying degrees of symptom relief and lowering of blood pressure after 10 to 30 days of treatment.

The clinical use of a chrysanthemum-flower decoction in treating 61 angina pectoris patients, with an overall positive response of 80%, was reported in 1973 in a Chinese research publication.

Home remedies: Chrysanthemum flowers are a popular home remedy in the Chinese household. A tea made by steeping them in boiling water (three to six flower heads per cup) is drunk for what

Cantonese call "feverish air" conditions. These are conditions characterized by one or more of the following: **headache** with a feeling of heaviness in the head; **dryness of the mouth; bitter taste in the mouth; bad breath;** and **dry, uncomfortable feeling in the throat.** This tea can be taken several times a day for several days, or until the "feverish air" disappears. I seldom take any drugs, but I do occasionally drink chrysanthemum tea, mainly for bad breath or a bitter taste in the mouth.

Another popular home remedy is for **tired** and **bloodshot eyes** due to excessive reading, close-range precision work, or other related factors. About 9 g. (0.3 oz.) of chrysanthemum flowers are steeped in boiling water for a few minutes. The liquid, which can be drunk, is decanted off, and the flower heads are used while still hot, though not so hot that they can burn the skin. The person afflicted lies down with eyes closed, and the flower heads are placed over the eyes and left there for 15 to 20 minutes. They are replaced with hot ones when they turn cold. Excess liquid can be drained or gently squeezed from the flower heads before each application. This treatment is usually done at night, immediately before bed.

There are many other recorded remedies employing chrysanthemum flowers, though most are in combination with other herbs. Their use in treating **skin disorders** is well documented, but for these conditions, chrysanthemum leaves (*ju hua ye* in Chinese) are considered superior. To treat these conditions, which include **skin sores, ulcers, boils, carbuncles,** and **inflammations,** fresh chrysanthemum leaves are usually used. They are made into a mash which is directly applied to the affected area. The juice from the leaves is also used, and is made by mashing the fresh leaves, then straining them; this juice is then painted onto the affected skin. Sometimes, when only dried leaves are available, they are ground into a powder which is then mixed with an adequate amount of water to form a mash or poultice.

Availability: Chrysanthemum flowers are commonly available in Chinese groceries and are served as a tea, if requested, in some Chinese restaurants in major Western cities. Florists' chrysanthemums are grown in many Western homes and gardens, and can serve as a source of fresh leaves.

COLTSFOOT

款冬

General information: Known botanically as *Tussilago farfara* of the composite family, coltsfoot is a common herb found in many parts of the world. It is generally considered to be a native of Eurasia and now also grows wild in North America and nontropical regions of China, where it is known as *kuan dong hua.* It is also cultivated in many of the temperate and northern Chinese provinces.

Coltsfoot is a perennial herb, 10 to 25 cm. (4–10 in.) high, with two types of leaves. The larger leaves rise from the creeping rootstock, and measure 7 to 15 cm. (2.8–5.9 in.) long and 8 to 16 cm. (3.1–6.3 in.) across, with long petioles (leafstalks) that are 8 to 20 cm. (3.1–7.9 in.) long. These leaves are heart- or egg-shaped and are held up by their long leafstalks. The leaf veins and leafstalks of those near the base of the plant are reddish and contain woolly hair. The flowering stem is also woolly, 5 to 20 cm. (2–7.9 in.) high, has 10 or more small scalelike alternate leaves and a yellow flower head. Unlike most herbs, coltsfoot flowers before sending up leaves. In China, it flowers in February or March and fruits in April.

For Chinese medicinal use, the flower heads are dug up before they emerge from the ground, in late October to late December. The buds are collected, rid of flowering stems and dirt, and dried in the shade.

Coltsfoot flowers contain steroids (e.g., faradiol), glycosides (e.g., rutin and hyperin), wax, volatile oil, tannins, taraxanthin, and other biologically active compounds.

The flowers and leaves of coltsfoot have been used in Western folk medicine for centuries to treat numerous respiratory conditions (e.g., coughs, colds, bronchitis, bronchial asthma, and hoarseness), diarrhea, insect bites, inflammations, and burns.

Effects on the body: In recent years, Chinese scientists have found a decoction of coltsfoot flowers to have antitussive (anti-cough), expectorant, and some anti-asthmatic effects in experimental animals such as mice, cats, and rabbits.

Traditional uses: Coltsfoot has been used in Chinese medicine for at least two thousand years, and is described in the Shennong Herbal. Traditionally, it is considered to taste pungent and to have warming, invigorating properties and to soothe the lungs, disperse phlegm, and stop coughs. It is used mainly in treating various lung or respiratory conditions, including coughs of long duration, difficulties in swallowing, and asthma. The usual daily internal dose is 1.6 to 9 g. (0.06–0.32 oz.), taken in the form of a decoction, powder, or pills.

Modern uses: In the past few decades, clinical use of extracts of coltsfoot flowers has been reported in Chinese medical and pharmaceutical journals.

A report from a journal of Chinese medicine from Shanghai describes the use of an alcoholic extract of coltsfoot in the treatment of wheezing. Each of 36 patients was given orally 5 ml. of the extract (equivalent to 6 g. of the dried flowers) three times a day. After taking this medicine, 19 of the patients responded—eight within two days. However, this preparation produced side effects that included nausea and insomnia.

In a report from another regional journal, an injection prepared from coltsfoot flowers and earthworms (also a standard Chinese medicine) was used in treating tracheitis (chronic inflammation of the trachea). Of 68 patients treated for 10 days continuously, all except four showed marked improvement or the disappearance of such symptoms as cough and wheezing. At the same time, appetite and sleep also improved. This preparation also significantly lowered patients' blood pressure.

Home remedies: Among several recipes recorded in classical herbals, only two appear relatively simple. They are described below.

To treat **wheezing, cough,** or **blood in sputum,** equal amounts of coltsfoot flowers and lily bulbs (*Lilium species,* a standard Chinese medicine) are ground to a fine powder, and mixed with honey to make pills the size of marbles. One pill a day is taken. The pill can be chewed and swallowed with ginger tea or it can be left in the mouth and allowed to dissolve slowly by itself. The latter method is said to give better results. This recipe is from a classical herbal of the mid-13th century. Essentially the same recipe is found in a modern practical herbal manual, except that a more precise dosage is given there: 9 g. (0.3 oz.) of pills are taken with boiled water twice daily.

In the same practical herbal manual, treatment of chronic **tracheitis** with incessant cough simply calls for placing honey-treated coltsfoot flowers in a pipe and smoking it. The honey-treated flowers are prepared by mixing five parts of flowers with one part of honey predissolved in a small amount of boiling water. The mixture is then fried until it is no longer sticky to the touch.

Availability: Coltsfoot grows in most of eastern North America, in clayey soil and near streams. The dried flower buds of coltsfoot are available from Chinese herb shops.

CORIANDER

芫荽

General information: Coriander is known in Chinese as *hu sui*—*hu,* meaning "foreign," denoting its foreign or, specifically, Western (that is, Middle Eastern and European) origin. It was introduced into China about two thousand years ago, during the Han Dynasty. It is also called *yan sui,* especially when used as a condiment. Botanically, coriander is *Coriandrum sativum* of the parsley family. It is native to Europe and western Asia, but is now cultivated in many other parts of the world, including North and South America and India.

The coriander plant is an annual herb, 0.3 to 1 m. (1–3 ft.) tall. It can be easily planted from seed in the spring. All parts of the coriander plant are used in food and in folk medicine (both Chinese and Western). The dried ripe fruits, commonly called coriander seeds, are used as a domestic spice and by the food industry in flavoring candy, baked goods, puddings, frozen dairy desserts, meat, and meat products. They are also one of the herbs used in flavoring gin and vermouths. Coriander oil is used in perfumes, soaps, creams, and lotions, and in flavoring tobacco and pharmaceutical preparations.

Known as cilantro in Spanish cuisine and as Chinese parsley in Chinese cooking, young coriander leaves come from a distinctly different plant than the common parsley one finds at vegetable stands, groceries, or supermarkets and have different properties and tastes. Most Americans and Europeans have probably come across coriander seeds on their spice shelves, and many have probably tasted coriander leaves in Chinese or Spanish dishes. However, few know that these condiments are from the same plant source.

Coriander seed contains usually about 1% volatile oil (coriander oil), up to 26% fats, 10% starch, 20% sugars, 12% protein, tannins, flavonoid glycosides, chlorogenic and caffeic acids, and many other biologically active constituents such as vitamins (e.g., niacin, riboflavin, and thiamine) and minerals (especially potassium and calcium).

Coriander leaves contain less volatile oil and less fats (5%), but more proteins (22%), than coriander seed. They also contain other active constituents similar to those in coriander seed.

Coriander seed has been used in Western folk medicine for several thousand years as an antispasmodic, appetite increaser, carminative, and stomachic. It is also used externally for rheumatism and painful joints.

Traditional uses: The first recorded use of coriander in Chinese medicine dates back to about A.D. 600. The whole herb (including roots) and the seed are used. Both are said to help digestion and to relieve measles.

Coriander herb (the whole herb, with root) is said to benefit the lungs and spleen. Its major uses include the treatment of measles (to accelerate its course), indigestion, and stomachache. But according to herbals of the 7th and 8th centuries A.D., long-term use of coriander herb adversely affects one's memory and vision. For internal use, it is generally boiled in water and the resulting liquid (decoction) is drunk. The usual daily dose is 9 to 15 g. (0.3–0.5 oz.) for the dried herb and 31 to 62 g. (1.1–2.2 oz.) for the fresh herb.

Ripe coriander seed, sun-dried, is said to stop bleeding, break up phlegm, and eliminate fish odors before and/or during cooking. Its primary uses include the treatment of hemorrhoids, smallpox, and (as with coriander herb) dysentery, measles, indigestion, constipation, and anal prolapse. It is also used for nausea, stomachache, and hernia; a decoction is used as a mouthwash to relieve toothache. The usual internal daily dose of coriander seed is 6 to 12 g. (0.2–0.4 oz.) taken as a decoction or as a powder. Externally, the decoction is used for gargling or washing.

Home remedies: To treat **toothache,** a mouthwash prepared from coriander seeds is used. About 9 g. (0.3 oz.) of seeds are boiled in 5 l. (5 qt.) of water down to about 1 l. (1 qt.) and the liquid is used for gargling as needed.

A Cantonese folk remedy for treating **bad breath, smelly urine,** or **female genital odor** calls for fresh coriander herb to be used in a soup. The soup is prepared like a typical Chinese vegetable soup. A small amount of meat (60 g., or 2 oz.) is boiled for a few minutes in two cups of water until it is just cooked. About 90 g. (3 oz.) of Chinese parsley with roots is added and boiled for a minute or two.

After seasoning (e.g., with salt and pepper), the soup and its contents are eaten. This remedy can be taken for a few days.

For treating **hemorrhoids,** 6 to 12 g. (0.2–0.4 oz.) of coriander seeds are stir heated in a frying pan until they turn brownish. They are then ground to a fine powder, mixed with wine, and the mixture is drunk.

Availability: Chinese parsley is available in most Chinese or other ethnic grocery stores. Coriander seed is available as a spice in spice shops and the spice sections of supermarkets.

CORN (Maize)

玉米须

General information: Corn, also known as Indian corn, sweet corn, or maize, and in South Africa as mealies, is now widely cultivated and consumed all over the world. The plant is generally considered to be a native of the New World and was cultivated by American Indians for many centuries. It is known scientifically as *Zea mays* of the grass family and exists in many cultivated varieties. An erect annual grass with most roots originating immediately above the surface of the ground, corn grows to a height of up to about 4 m. (13 ft.). It is cultivated mainly for its kernels, which are used either as a vegetable when young or as cereal grain or animal feed when fully mature. Since it is easy to grow, corn is often grown in home gardens. The corn kernels are borne on a corncob, and kernels and cob together are known as an ear of corn. Corn silk consists of the long and slender styles and stigmas of the pistils. It sticks out from the tip of an ear of corn like a beard; in Chinese it is known as *yu mi xu,* or "corn beard." Corn silk can reach as much as 30 cm. (1 ft.) in length. It is used either fresh or dried—normally sun-dried.

Corn silk contains about 1% bitter glycosides, 3% saponins, 0.1% to 0.2% volatile oil, 2.5% fats, 2.7% resin, 1% tannin, vitamins C and K, steroids (e.g., sitosterol and stigmasterol), alkaloids, allantoin, and others.

Long used in American folk medicine as a diuretic and demulcent (unguent), corn silk (usually in extract form) is an ingredient in some diuretic preparations sold over the counter in America and Europe. It has also been used traditionally for inflammatory conditions such as cystitis and pyelitis and was formerly an officially recognized drug in the United States. In cosmetics, its powdered form is used in face powders. Corn-silk extracts are also used as a flavoring ingredient in processed food products in the West.

Effects on the body: Most of the pharmacological research on corn silk has been reported by Chinese and Japanese scientists. They have found that corn silk can lower the blood pressure and blood sugar levels of experimental animals (e.g., rabbits and dogs). A water extract of corn silk has been found to be strongly diuretic in humans and in rabbits, with very low toxic effects. Thus, with intravenous injection, only 1.5 mg./kg. was required for diuretic effects in rabbits, while 250 mg./kg. produced fatal results in these animals.

Traditional uses: Although the earliest recorded uses of other corn products (kernels, leaves, and roots) in Chinese medicine date back to the latter part of the 16th century, the first recorded medicinal use of corn silk did not appear until only a few decades ago. Corn silk is listed as an official drug in the pharmacopeia of the People's Republic of China and is used as a diuretic and hypotensive in the treatment of edema, nephritis (kidney inflammation), urinary difficulties, jaundice, and hypertension. Traditionally, it is also used for diabetes, hepatitis, kidney stones, gallstones, cholecystitis (gallbladder inflammation), beriberi, chylous hematuria (milky and bloody urine), and hematemesis (vomiting blood). The usual internal daily dose is 15 to 30 g. (0.5–1 oz.), but at times up to 60 g. (2.1 oz.); it is normally taken as a decoction.

Corncob is used in treating edema, urinary difficulties, beriberi, and diarrhea. It contains a polysaccharide (made of simple sugars) that has been shown to inhibit the growth of experimentally induced tumors in mice. Corncob is usually taken internally as a decoction, with a usual daily dose of 90 to 150 g. (3.2–5.3 oz.).

Corn kernels are seldom used in medicine. They are considered a nutrient and to have appetite-stimulating properties.

Corn leaves are used mainly for treating urinary stones. Like corncob, they also contain an antitumor polysaccharide. The usual daily dose of fresh corn leaves for urinary stones is 62 g. (2.2 oz.), taken in the form of a decoction.

Corn roots are also used for treating urinary stones. The usual daily dose of the fresh roots is also 62 g. (2.2 oz.), taken as a decoction.

Modern uses: During the past few decades, the Chinese have been applying modern scientific methods in using and evaluating Chinese herbal drugs. Reports of the successful use of corn silk in treating chronic nephritis and nephrotic syndrome have appeared in Chinese medical journals. For example, in one report, which appeared in 1960 in the *Chinese Journal of Internal Medicine,* it was recorded that, of 12 patients with nephrotic syndrome treated by corn silk, edema completely disappeared in nine patients and mostly disappeared in two others, after three months of treatment. Ten of the patients had had severe edema all over their bodies before treatment. The treatment consisted of giving the patients a decoction of 60 g. (2.1 oz.) of dried corn silk twice daily, once in the morning and once at night. At the same time, the patients were given 1 g. of potassium chloride three time a day. One patient's edema disappeared in 15 days, the shortest time observed.

Home remedies: There are many home remedies based on corn products. Most of these call for corn silk and are of relatively recent origin.

However, in the 16th century, Li Shizhen, in his famous herbal *Ben Cao Gang Mu,* gives the first recorded remedy for urinary stones which calls for corn leaves or corn roots. He writes, "For **urinary stones** that cause unbearable pain, make a decoction of corn leaves or corn roots and drink it often." In modern practical herbals, the daily doses of fresh corn leaves or roots are given as 62 to 124 g. (2.2–4.4 oz.).

To treat **high blood pressure,** 31 g. (1.1 oz.) of dried corn silk is boiled slowly in two cups of water until about one cup remains. The boiling takes about 40 minutes. The liquid is strained off and is taken once daily. This remedy appears in numerous Chinese practical herbals and is also used for treating **diabetes** and **nephritic edema.**

For **nephritis** or early **kidney stones,** another remedy also calls for frequently drinking a decoction of corn silk.

Availability: Corn silk can be obtained from the fresh ears of corn that are readily available at fruit and vegetable stands, supermarkets, and groceries, when corn is in season. It can be used fresh or dried for later use. Dried corn silk is also available in Chinese herb shops.

Corncobs can be saved after corn kernels are consumed.

Corn leaves and roots can be obtained from home gardens or from farm and fruit and vegetable stands.

CUCUMBER

黄瓜

General information: Common throughout the world, cucumbers are consumed raw, cooked, and pickled, or in other ways. Westerners like them raw in salads and rarely eat them cooked, but peoples in the Far East, especially the Chinese, usually eat them cooked. When I was a child, my family only occasionally ate cucumber raw, and always after it had been meticulously washed, because of an age-old Chinese tradition of avoiding raw foods for hygienic reasons. Even though I have lived in America for more than 20 years and have gotten used to Western conditions, I still feel uneasy whenever I eat a salad, especially outside of my home, as in a restaurant.

Known scientifically as *Cucumis sativus* of the gourd family, the cucumber plant is an annual herb that grows by trailing along the ground or by climbing a support. It is believed to be native to Asia, probably the Middle East. According to Chinese records, cucumber was introduced to China around 100 B.C. (during the Han Dynasty) from countries to the west by way of what later became known as the Silk Route, later taken by Marco Polo. For six to seven hundred years, cucumber bore the name *hu gua,* meaning "foreign melon," but a later name, *huang gua,* meaning "yellow melon," is now more commonly used.

Numerous varieties of the plant produce fruits (cucumbers) of different sizes, shapes, colors, and flavors. They are easy to grow and, depending on the variety, range in shape from nearly round (rare) to elongate (common), and in taste from nonbitter to quite bitter, especially at the stem tips. Some cucumbers of the elongate type can reach 1 m. (3 ft.) in length, but most are between 10 cm. (4 in.) and 30 cm. (1 ft.) long.

Like most vegetables and fruits, raw cucumbers contain large amounts of water (95%). The rest is made up of about 1% protein, 3% carbohydrates, minor amounts of fats (0.1%), minerals, and vitamins (e.g., A, Bs, and C), none in unusually high concentration. Cucumbers also contain minor amounts of numerous other biologically active constituents. Their bitter taste is due to compounds known as cucurbitacins, one of which has been found to have antitumor effects on experimental animals.

In Western folk medicine, cucumber is considered a diuretic and a laxative. Externally, the juice is said to be good for soothing skin inflammations, burns, and irritations, and for treating freckles and wrinkles.

Traditional uses: The first recorded medicinal use of the cucumber was in the 7th century. In Chinese medicine, cucumber is considered to have heat-dissipating, diuretic, laxative, and detoxifying effects. Its major uses include the treatment of excessive thirst, sore throat, laryngitis, acute conjunctivitis, and burns. In most Chinese homes, however, whether eaten raw or cooked as a soup, cucumber is used only for keeping cool in summer, when it is in season, or in early autumn to soothe dry lips and throat.

The leaves, roots, and stems are also used in Chinese medicine: the leaves and roots for diarrhea and dysentery; the stems for dysentery, urinary disorders, and sores. Both fresh and dried forms are used. The leaves and roots are collected in the summer or fall and are sun-dried. The stems are collected in early summer before or at the time of flowering and are dried in the shade.

While the medicinal uses of cucumber stems are of relatively recent origin (18th century), the first recorded uses of cucumber leaves and cucumber roots date back to the 8th and 16th centuries respectively. They are used both internally (as a decoction) and externally (as a mash), with internal doses for roots and stems of 28 to 56 g. (1–2 oz.) daily. The traditional dose for the leaves is one leaf for a one-year-old child. (Presumably more for older children or adults—but this is not stated.)

Modern uses: Cucumber stems have recently been used clinically in China for treating high blood pressure. Their effectiveness is described in a report of 1973 in which 53 of 64 patients with hypertension responded when treated with tablets of dried cucumber stems. The treatment consisted of taking 12.5 g. (0.4 oz.) of tablets three times daily for one to two months. Side effects were minimal. Only five of the patients experienced a burning sensation in the stomach after taking the tablets; this was reduced or disappeared when the patients took the tablets after meals.

In a report of 1972, decoctions or extracts of cucumber seedlings (with roots and leaves removed) were also effective in treating high blood pressure. Of 62 patients thus treated, 54 responded, half with their blood pressure down in the normal range.

Home remedies: One of the more popular home remedies for treating **dryness of lips and throat** and preventing **laryngitis** or sore throat in late summer and early fall is to use a soup prepared from old, well-ripened cucumbers. The soup is prepared just like a regular vegetable soup and drunk often during this period.

In a traditional remedy for treating painful acute **conjunctivitis,** a well-ripened cucumber is used. A hole is made at one end and the seeds and pulp are removed. It is then filled with Glauber's salt (sodium sulfate). After the hole is sealed, the filled cucumber is hung in the shade for some weeks until white crystals accumulate on the surface. The crystals are then scraped off and used to prepare a solution for eye drops.

Availability: Cucumbers are sold at groceries and in supermarkets. The leaves, roots, and stems of the cucumber plant can be obtained from home gardens.

DANDELION

蒲公英

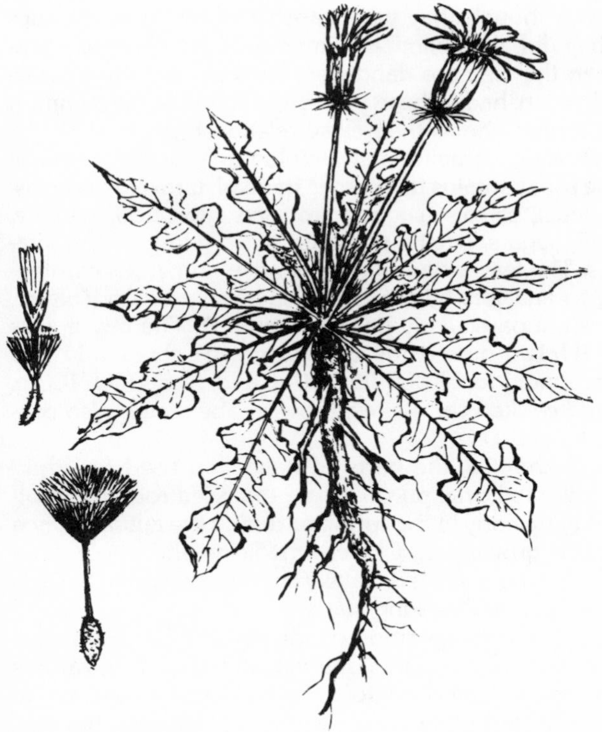

General information: There are many related species of dandelion, known collectively as *Taraxacum,* belonging to the composite family. The common dandelion, scientifically called *Taraxacum officinale,* is a native of Europe and is now widespread throughout Europe and North America. Most gardeners consider it a weed and a pest. Its Chinese counterpart is *Taraxacum mongolicum,* which is distributed in most regions of China, where the dandelion is known as *pu gong ying.* Besides these two species, many others are also used in folk medicine.

The common dandelion and the Chinese dandelion are both hardy perennial herbs, about 25 to 45 cm. (10–18 in.) high, with the former larger than the latter. They have deep roots and deeply cut lanceolate leaves that form rosettes arising at ground level. Their yellow flower heads are borne on long stalks, one or more per plant. Both types of dandelion contain a white milky juice throughout the plant.

Western scientists have done extensive chemical research on the common dandelion during the past 70 years. The Chinese, however, didn't bother to analyze the Chinese dandelion chemically until about 10 years ago, even though they were capable of doing so decades earlier. When they did, the chemical compounds the Chinese scientists discovered in the Chinese dandelion, such as choline, taraxasterol, inulin, and pectin, had all been previously found in the common dandelion. This further shows their close relationship.

Common dandelion contains many biologically active chemical constituents. The root contains triterpenes (taraxol, taraxerol, taraxasterol, β-amyrin, etc.), sterols (stigmasterol and sitosterol), choline, about 25% inulin, sugars, pectin, phenolic acids, gums, resins, vitamins, and others. The leaves and flowers contain numerous carotenoids. According to analyses by the U.S. Department of Agriculture, dandelion greens are particularly rich in vitamin A. The raw greens contain 14,000 IU/100 g. and the cooked greens contain 11,700 IU/100 g., as compared to 11,000 IU/100 g. and 10,500 IU/100 g. present in raw and cooked carrots respectively. The greens also contain vitamins B, C, and D.

In Europe and America, the parts of dandelion used for pharmaceutical and folk medicinal purposes are the dried root and rootstock. They are dug up early in the spring or during the autumn when they are not actively growing. In Chinese medicine, the whole dried herb (greens and roots) is used. It is usually collected in spring or early summer before or just as flowering starts.

In Western folk medicine common dandelion root has been used for centuries as a laxative, tonic, and diuretic, and in treating various liver, gallbladder, and kidney conditions. Its extracts are used extensively in pharmaceutical preparations (e.g., tonic, laxative, diuretic, and antismoking) as well as in processed food products, where they serve as flavoring agents. Roasted dandelion root and its extracts are used as coffee substitutes themselves or in instant-coffee substitute preparations. Dandelion greens are used in salad or as vegetables, and dandelion flowers in domestic winemaking. In short, the whole dandelion plant is useful, and one should not consider it a mere weed or pest.

Effects on the body: Chinese scientists have found that the juice expressed from fresh Chinese dandelion herb and extracts of dandelion herb strongly inhibit the growth of numerous kinds of bacteria.

Allergic reactions (e.g., contact dermatitis) to common dandelion have been reported.

Traditional uses: Dandelion's use in traditional Chinese medicine was first recorded in the middle of the 7th century, during the Tang Dynasty. According to one of the herbals *(Tang Ben Cao)* of that period, dandelion . . . "has yellow flowers, produces a white juice when broken, and is eaten by everyone." It must have been a common vegetable at that time.

Traditionally, dandelion is considered to taste both bitter and sweet and to have cooling properties. It has the ability to dissipate heat, reduce inflammation, and detoxify the body. Officially recognized in the pharmacopeia of the People's Republic of China, Chinese dandelion is used for treating acute mastitis, carbuncles and sores, chronic gastritis, and urinary-tract infections. Other conditions for which it is also used include hepatitis, acute bronchitis, acute tonsillitis, colds with fever, and parotiditis (mumps). The usual daily internal dose is 9 to 31 g. (0.3–1.1 oz.) taken as a decoction. The quantity is doubled if fresh herb is used.

Modern uses: In recent years, the traditionally acknowledged detoxifying and heat-dissipating ("cold") qualities of Chinese dandelion have been interpreted as its ability to counter infections. Many reports appearing in Chinese medical and pharmaceutical journals (both national and regional) have described successful clinical uses of Chinese dandelion in treating various infections. It has been used in the form of powdered herb, water extract, alcoholic extract, and fresh juice, being most effective in treating upper respiratory tract infections, acute and chronic bronchitis, pneumonia, infectious hepatitis, urinary-tract infections, acute mastitis, acute pancreatitis, appendicitis, and dermatitis, and in preventing postoperative infections. It replaced modern antibiotics in some applications, with the advantage of causing fewer side effects. Any side effects that occurred, such as stomach upset or dizziness, disappeared completely when the dandelion treatment was stopped.

Home remedies: Many remedies based on Chinese dandelion are recorded in traditional as well as modern herbals. Most of the recipes contain multiple herbs. The following are a few of the simpler ones. If Chinese dandelion is not available, the common dandelion is a reasonable substitute, as the two are similar in many respects. However, unless otherwise specified, the whole herb of the common dandelion should be used.

A recipe in a modern practical herbal for treating **mastitis** calls for simply boiling 31 g. (1.1 oz.) dandelion in three large cups of water until one to one-and-a-half cups remain and drinking the resulting liquid after decanting or straining off the residue. This recipe is also used for treating **cholecystitis (gallbladder inflammation).**

To treat **mumps,** a recipe in the same herbal calls for boiling 15 g. (0.5 oz.) of dandelion in two cups of water until they are reduced to about one cup. After decanting or straining off the solids, the liquid is drunk.

According to a traditional recipe, nasty **sores** of long duration and **snake or insect bites** can be treated by mashing fresh dandelion and applying the mash directly to the affected areas.

A modern recipe for treating stomach and duodenal **ulcers** calls for use of dandelion root. The root is ground to a powder, which is taken three times daily after meals. The dose each time is 1.5 g. (0.05 oz.).

A Cantonese home remedy for treating **bloodshot eyes** (not due to drinking or lack of sleep) makes use of dandelion and cicada shells (also a common Chinese drug). Sixty-two grams (2.2 oz.) of fresh dandelion and 6 g. (0.2 oz.) of cicada shells are gently boiled in three large cups of water until about one-and-a-half cups remain. Each night, one cup of the decoction is drunk. The remainder is used externally: a wad of cotton wetted with the decoction is placed directly over closed eyes. The cotton is kept wet with the liquid for a period of about 30 minutes. This treatment is said to take effect in a few days. It is also used for **inflammation of the eyes** (eyeballs and conjunctiva).

Availability: Chinese dandelion is available in Chinese herb shops. Fresh common dandelion can be found anywhere outdoors (lawns, meadows, waste places, etc.).

DILL

蒔蘿子

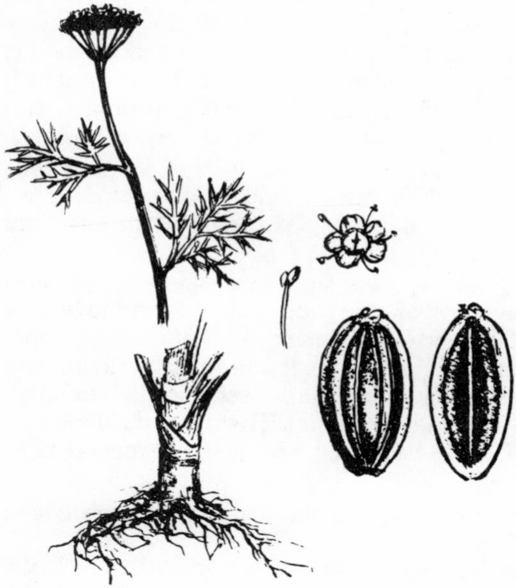

General information: The dill plant is an annual or biennial herb with a smooth and erect stem, up to about 1 m. (3.3 ft.) high. Its leaves are finely dissected, like branches of needles. Dill is scientifically called *Anethum graveolens* of the parsley family and is known in Chinese as *shi luo zi* or *xiao hui xiang* ("small fennel"). It is a native of the Mediterranean and southern Russia and is cultivated in European countries as well as in the United States, the West Indies, India, and China. The dried ripe fruit (dill seed) and the whole aboveground herb (dill herb) furnish the well-known spices. They are also used for the production of dill-seed oil and dill-herb oil, both of which are used as flavor or fragrance components in food, drug, and cosmetic products in Western countries.

For Chinese medicine, the dill fruits are harvested by collecting the whole of the fruiting branches (umbels). After drying under the sun, these are thrashed to release the fruits, which, after being separated from extraneous matter, are further sun-dried to yield the dill seed.

Dill seed usually contains 2.5% to 4% volatile oil, composed mainly of carvone with lesser amounts of numerous other aromatic chemicals. Dill also contains coumarins (e.g., bergapten, scopoletin, and umbelliferone), steroids (e.g., sitosterol), flavonoids, glucosides, phenolic acids, about 16% protein, 15% fats, 55% carbohydrates, minerals (especially calcium and potassium) and vitamins (e.g., A and C), among other constituents.

In Western folk medicine, dill seed is used as an antispasmodic, sedative, carminative, diuretic, and stomachic. Conditions for which it is used include lack of appetite, upset stomach, insomnia, and flatulence. It is also used to promote milk flow in nursing mothers.

Effects on the body: Dill-seed oil has been the subject of various experiments with animals and has been found to lower blood pressure, inhibit the growth of bacteria, and relax spasms of the intestines and uterine muscles.

Traditional uses: Dill seed is considered in Chinese medicine to taste pungent and to have invigorating properties. It is said to benefit the spleen, kidney, and stomach—dispersing colds, increasing appetite, and getting rid of fish and meat toxins. It is used mainly in treating gastrointestinal problems, including stomachache, colic, vomiting, lack of appetite, and abdominal distention. The usual daily internal dose is 2.5 to 5 g. (0.1–0.2 oz.) taken in the form of a decoction, pills, or powder.

Home remedies: The following are three remedies reproduced from classical herbals.

To treat **abdominal distention, vomiting, inability to hold food,** and **flank pain** in children, a well-known 15th-century book of remedies directs one to make pills the size of mung beans (or peas) out of dill-seed powder. For a three-year-old child, 30 pills are given with tangerine-peel tea. For adults, the dose is of course larger.

To treat **backache** due to sudden sprain, 6 g. (0.2 oz.) of dill seed powder is taken with wine.

For treating **hernia,** and **"painful abdominal mass"** in women, 38 g. (1.3 oz.) of dill seed is roasted (fried) until brown, ground to a powder, and taken with wine.

Availability: Dill seed is readily available as a spice in grocery stores and supermarkets.

FENNEL

茴香

General information: Fennel seed is used in Western countries primarily as a spice. Although it is sometimes so used in China, its main use there is as a medicinal herb. Fennel seed is derived from a perennial herb known scientifically as *Foeniculum vulgare* of the parsley family. Its Chinese name is *xiao hui xiang,* or simply *hui xiang, xiao* meaning "small" and *hui xiang* meaning "restoring flavor." Each seed is about the size and shape of a grain of rice. The plant is 1 to 1.5 m. (3–5 ft.) tall and is a native of the Mediterranean region. It now grows wild and is also cultivated in many countries, including the United States, Great Britain, and China. When cultivated, it is usually an annual or biennial plant.

Fennel seed generally contains 2% to 6% volatile oil (fennel oil), 17% to 20% fats, 16% to 20% proteins, vitamins (it is relatively high in vitamin E), minerals (especially calcium and potassium), and other active constituents. Like star-anise oil, fennel oil is made up mostly of anethole. It also contains many other aromatic chemical compounds.

Fennel seed and fennel oil are used in many processed food products in the West. Fennel oil is also used as a carminative or flavoring agent in some laxative preparations, and for scenting soaps, lotions, creams, detergents, and perfumes.

In Western folk medicine, fennel seed is used as a carminative, stomachic, expectorant, and diuretic, among other things. Conditions for which it is used include flatulence and other stomach troubles, coughing, loss of appetite, and colic.

Effects on the body: Fennel oil, like star-anise oil, can cause skin allergies, irritations, or dermatitis in certain sensitive individuals. It also has been shown to have muscle-relaxing, antibacterial, and insecticidal properties.

Traditional uses: In the Far East, especially in the warmer regions, spices are often used to mask the flavor of food that has gone off. According to a 6th-century Chinese herbal, fennel got the name "restoring flavor" because it could restore the original flavor (aroma) of meat that had turned. This was accomplished by cooking the meat with a small amount of fennel seeds.

Fennel has been used in Chinese medicine for many centuries. Its first recorded use appeared in a 6th-century herbal. Seed, root, leaf, and stem are all used, and their uses are generally similar.

Fennel seed is said to warm the kidneys and to calm the stomach as well as benefit the bladder. It is used to treat conditions similar to those treated with star anise, including hernia, indigestion, bellyache, lumbago due to kidney deficiencies, stomachache, nausea, and vomiting. Other uses include the treatment of swollen testicles, painful menstrual periods, bed-wetting, cholera, and hard-to-heal snakebites. It is one of the official drugs listed in the pharmacopeia of the People's Republic of China, with a usual daily dose of 3 to 9 g. (0.1–0.3 oz.) taken as a tea, decoction, or powder.

Modern uses: One of the best-known traditional uses of fennel seed is in the treatment of hernia of the small intestine. In recent years, its effectiveness for this condition has been confirmed in several Chinese national and regional medical journals. Thus, for treating incarcerated hernia of the small intestine, a tea made with 9 to 15 g. (0.3–0.5 oz.) fennel seed was drunk while hot. The patient then lay on his back with legs together and knees half-bent. If no response was observed in 15 to 30 minutes the same dose could be repeated again. Generally, the hernia receded and pain disappeared about 30 minutes after treatment. Patients who did not respond one hour after this treatment had to undergo surgery. In one report, of 26 patients treated by this method, only four did not respond. The patients had hernias ranging from two hours to three days in duration. Those with hernias of short duration responded better than those with hernias of longer duration.

Home remedies: Herbals have recorded many remedies using fennel seed, most in combination with other herbs. Two simpler examples are cited here.

To treat hard-to-heal **snakebites,** a 7th-century remedy calls for simply applying a poultice of fennel seed directly on the wounded area.

To treat **stomachache** with digestive difficulties, a remedy from a modern practical herbal calls for mashing 56 g. (2 oz.) of fennel seed with 112 g. (4 oz.) of fresh ginger root, frying or roasting the mixture until brownish, and grinding it to a powder. The powder is taken with rice soup. The dose is 3 g. (0.1 oz.), three times a day.

Availability: Fennel seed is available as a spice in groceries, supermarkets, and other food stores.

GARDEN BALSAM

凤仙

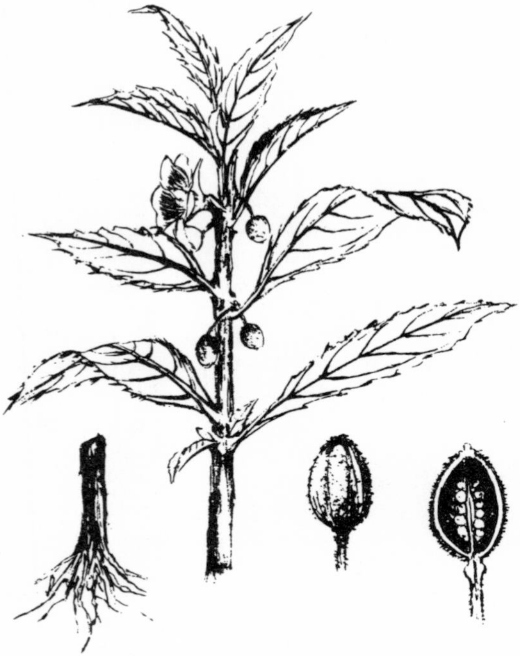

General information: Also known as impatiens or simply as balsam, garden balsam is a member of the touch-me-not family whose ripe pods burst suddenly when they are touched, expelling the seeds. Botanically, garden balsam is called *Impatiens balsamina.* In Chinese, garden-balsam herb (the whole plant) is called *feng xian,* which means "phoenix fairy," referring to its phoenixlike flowers. Garden-balsam flowers are known by numerous names. Two of the most common are *feng xian hua* ("phoenix fairy flower") and *zhi jia hua* ("fingernail flower"), the latter referring to the use of garden-balsam flowers by Chinese women for dyeing their fingernails. It is also the Chinese name for henna. (Both garden balsam and henna contain a pigment called lawsone.) Garden-balsam seeds are called *ji xing zi,* meaning "short temper," which probably refers to the manner in which the seeds burst out of the ripe pods when disturbed.

Garden balsam is a stout annual, up to about 90 cm. (3 ft.) tall, with juicy stems that range in texture from smooth to hairy. Its flowers, borne at the junctions between leaf and stem, are usually pink or red, but can range in color from white to purple, or mixed. Garden-balsam flowers in summer and fruits in early autumn. The brown seeds are roundish or egg-shaped, with a diameter of about 2 mm. Garden balsam is a native of Asia (e.g., China and India). It is now cultivated worldwide as an ornamental plant and exists in numerous varieties. The whole herb—its flowers, seeds, and roots—is used in traditional Chinese medicine. The dried stems and seeds are officially listed in the pharmacopeia of the People's Republic of China.

Although some chemical analyses have been done on its flowers and seeds, not much is known about the active constituents of garden balsam. The flowers contain pigments, such as anthocyanins, most of which are typical of flowers of other plants. The seeds contain proteins, sugars, fats, amino acids, steroids, saponins, and volatile oil, among other constituents, many of which are also typical of plant seeds in general.

Although a widely used medicinal herb in China, garden balsam has not attracted much attention in the West other than as an ornamental plant. However, one of its relatives, the jewelweed *(Impatiens biflora),* is quite well known as a remedy for poison-ivy irritations. For these purposes, the juice of the plant is applied directly to the irritated areas.

Effects on the body: During the past few decades, Chinese scientists have found that water extracts of garden-balsam flowers inhibit the growth of fungi that cause certain ringworms. Water extracts of balsam flowers can also stop the growth of pathogenic (disease-causing) bacteria such as *Staphylococcus aureus* and *Streptococcus pyogenes,* the latter causing what commonly are called "strep infections." These scientists have also found that alcoholic and water extracts of garden-balsam seeds stimulate the uterus of experimental animals. Decoctions of garden-balsam seeds have also been shown to have contraceptive effects on female mice.

Traditional uses: Garden balsam, in various forms, has been used in Chinese medicine for centuries. The first record of its medicinal use dates back to the 14th century.

Garden-balsam herb is collected during the summer and autumn. It is considered to have the ability to dispel toxins that cause rheumatism and colds, promote blood circulation, stop pain, and reduce swelling. It is regarded as bitter and pungent-tasting, and nontoxic to slightly toxic in nature. Conditions for which garden-balsam herb is most often used include arthritic pain due to rheumatism, traumatic injuries, scrofula, boils, sores, and carbuncles. The usual internal daily dose is 9 to 15 g. (0.3–0.5 oz.) of dried herb or 31 to 62 g. (1.1–2.2 oz.) of fresh herb, taken as a decoction. Externally, a decoction is used to wash affected areas; alternatively, the fresh herb can be mashed and applied directly.

Garden-balsam flowers are collected during the flowering season, in the afternoon, and sun-dried. Red and white flowers are considered superior to other colors. Garden-balsam flowers have the same medicinal qualities as the whole herb and are used for treating similar conditions. The usual internal daily dose is 1.5 to 3 g. (0.05–0.1 oz.) of dried flowers or 3 to 9 g. (0.1–0.3 oz.) of fresh flowers. They are generally taken as a decoction, straight powder, or powder in wine. For external use the fresh flowers are usually mashed and directly applied to the affected areas, or the decoction is used as a wash.

Garden-balsam roots also have qualities and uses similar to those of the whole herb. In addition, for centuries they have been used to soften bones (e.g., fish bones) that are lodged in the throat. For internal use, the dried roots are usually ground into a powder which is taken with a swallow of wine; the daily dose is 9 to 15 g. (0.3–0.5 oz.). For external use, the fresh roots are mashed and applied directly to the affected areas.

Garden-balsam seeds are collected when the seed pods are almost ripe and not yet opened. The pods are then dried under the sun and the seeds are separated. The seeds are also considered to have medicinal qualities similar to those of the whole herb. Like the roots, the seeds are said to soften bones, and also teeth. According to Li Shizhen, the famous 16th-century herbalist, cooks used to add a few seeds to bony fish during cooking to make it tender. He also advises one to rinse one's mouth with warm water after taking garden-balsam seeds or roots to avoid damage to one's teeth by prolonged contact with them. Major uses of balsam seeds are for dislodging bones from one's throat and for treating swallowing difficulties, amenorrhea, and indigestion (especially in children).

(The Chinese eat fish frequently, and many of the fish they eat are very bony. They can usually deftly separate the meat from the fine bones with their teeth, lips, tongue, and chopsticks. However, accidents do sometimes occur, especially with children. Whenever a bone is lodged in the throat it can usually be dislodged physically by swallowing a mouthful of rice without chewing it first. When this method fails, others are tried. I remember as a child I used to have my share of this kind of accident, and needed no more drastic treatment than a few swallows of unchewed rice.)

Garden-balsam seeds are taken boiled in water, or in the form of a powder or pills washed down with water. Externally, the powdered seeds are applied directly to affected areas. The usual internal daily dose is 2.5 to 6 g. (0.1–0.2 oz.).

Home remedies: There is no lack of traditional home remedies based on garden balsam, and many of these using garden balsam alone are recorded in classical as well as modern practical herbals. A few examples follow.

To treat pain due to **articular rheumatism,** a modern herbal from Fujian (a southeastern province of China) calls for simply boiling 31 g. (1.1 oz.) of fresh garden-balsam herb in water. The resulting liquid is taken mixed with wine.

To treat **scrofula** and **carbuncles** (especially those on the back), a folk remedy from Jiangxi (a southeastern province) utilizes the fresh herb in two different ways. It is either mashed and applied directly to the scrofula or carbuncle, or it is boiled in water. For the latter, the whole herb is mashed and placed in a copper pot. Water is then added and the mixture is boiled for 20 to 30 minutes. The resulting liquid is strained or filtered through a clean cloth. More water is added to the residue and again boiled. The second filtrate is combined with the first, and the mixture is boiled down to a sticky consistency. This sticky extract is spread on clean paper or cloth and is placed directly on the affected areas. It is replaced each day with fresh material.

For treating unbearable **pain around the lower torso or waist,** a recipe in Li Shizhen's *Ben Cao Gang Mu* calls for sun-dried garden-balsam flowers ground into a powder. When pain occurs, 9 g. (0.3 oz.) of the powder is taken with wine on an empty stomach once daily.

A folk remedy from Guizhou (a southern province) for relieving **pain** is worth mentioning. In China, and in Hong Kong, when a person has a broken bone, he does not usually consult a Western physician or orthopedist. Rather, he consults a Chinese physician specializing in mending bones and healing wounds. This physician resets the broken bone between simple splints, which allow the patient to move with much freedom, in contrast to the plaster casts favored by Western orthopedists. Sometimes a broken bone causes such severe pain that resetting it is impossible. To relieve the pain, 3 g. (0.1 oz.) dried or 9 g. (0.3 oz.) fresh garden-balsam flowers soaked in wine are taken internally. About one hour after taking this remedy, the injured area will be numb and thus ready for resetting.

To treat **whooping cough, spitting blood,** or **coughing blood,** a Fujian folk remedy calls for taking seven to 15 garden-balsam flowers boiled in water. Boiling the flowers with a small amount of rock candy is said to produce even better results.

To treat **fungus infection of the hand** simply mash fresh balsam flowers and apply directly.

A recipe for treating **bones** (chicken, fish, etc.) **lodged in the throat** is recorded in a 14th-century book of remedies based on the author's experience as the member of a family who had been physicians for five successive generations. This recipe calls for chewing and swallowing garden-balsam roots or seeds. In order not to harm the teeth, the patient rinses with warm water following treatment. Alternatively, the seeds can be crushed and taken with water.

According to a modern practical herbal, **menstruation difficulties** can be treated by pills combining honey with garden-balsam seed. The pills are prepared by mixing 94 g. (3.3 oz.) of ground seed with an adequate amount of hot honey. The pills are divided into 30 equal groups, and one is taken three times a day with tea made from 9 g. (0.3 oz.) of *dang gui* (*Angelica sinensis* root).

Availability: Fresh garden-balsam herb, flowers, seeds, and roots can be obtained from home gardens. The dried herb, flowers, seeds, and roots are available from Chinese herb shops.

GARLIC

大蒜

General information: The beneficial qualities of garlic have been described in many Western books and articles. Indeed, if not for the odors it generates, garlic could become as common a household drug item as aspirin.

Garlic is known scientifically as *Allium sativum* of the lily family. It is known in Chinese as *da suan* and has also been called *hu suan,* with *hu* denoting its Western origin (see Coriander). It is a strong-scented perennial herb with long, flat, firm leaves that can be as broad as 2.5 cm. (1 in.). Its flowering stem can reach 1.2 m. (4 ft.) high. Its bulb has several parts, or cloves, all enclosed in a thin, white or purplish membranelike skin, and measures up to 3 cm. (1.2 in.) or more thick. Garlic is a native of Europe and Central Asia and now also grows in North America and other parts of the world. It is cultivated worldwide primarily for use as a condiment. The bulbs are collected in the summer after the leaves have withered and are dried in the shade, if necessary.

Fresh garlic contains about 0.2% volatile oil (garlic oil), alliin, alliinase (an enzyme that breaks down alliin), minerals (e.g., calcium, phosphorus, iron, and potassium), and vitamins (e.g., thiamine, riboflavin, niacin, and C), among other constituents. According to a report by the Chinese Academy of Medical Sciences, Chinese garlic contains 70% water, 23% carbohydrates, 4.4% proteins, 1.3% ash, 0.7% fiber, and 0.2% fats. By comparison, according to U.S. Department of Agriculture figures, American garlic contains 61.3% water, 30.8% carbohydrates, 6.2% proteins, 1.5% ash, 1.5% fiber, and 0.2% fats. The vitamin and mineral contents of American garlic are also generally higher than those of Chinese garlic.

Garlic oil contains allicin and other sulfur-containing compounds such as allylpropyl disulfide, diallyl disulfide, and diallyl trisulfide. Allicin is responsible for much of the pungent odor and taste of garlic. It is generated by the action of the enzyme alliinase on alliin. Under normal conditions, alliinase and alliin are separated from each other inside the garlic bulb. However, when the bulb is cut or crushed, the two are brought together and alliinase turns alliin (a nonvolatile odorless sulfur amino acid) into allicin (a pungent volatile sulfur compound).

Garlic has long been used in Western folk medicine for treating various ills, including arteriosclerosis, high blood pressure, colds, coughs, chronic bronchitis, earache, toothache, hysteria, dandruff, and pinworms.

In addition to their use in cooking, fresh and powdered dried garlic, along with garlic oil, are also used extensively in seasoning all sorts of processed food and drink products in the Western world.

Effects on the body: Garlic has a wide variety of biological effects which have been described in many scientific reports from both the West and the East. Although not all the active chemical constituents of garlic are known, the volatile, sulfur-containing compounds, especially allicin, diallyl disulfide, and diallyl trisulfide, are generally considered to be responsible for most of the biological effects of garlic. Allicin, at a concentration of only 1 in 100,000 (or one-thousandth of 1%) inhibits the growth of various bacteria, fungi, and disease-causing amoebas.

It is now well known that garlic (oil, juice, or extract) has antibacterial and antifungal qualities, being inhibitory to some microbes and deadly to others. It also kills amoebas that cause amebic dysentery and trichomonads that cause trichomoniasis (a vaginal parasitic infestation).

Both Western and Eastern scientists have found that garlic and its water extract, when given to rats and mice by injection or in their feed, inhibit the growth, or prevent the formation, of experimentally induced tumors in these animals. Researchers have also found that garlic and garlic oil lower the blood-sugar level in rabbits, blood cholesterol in rabbits and humans, and blood pressure in animals and humans as well as preventing the formation of arteriosclerosis.

Despite its many beneficial qualities, garlic also induces blisters, irritation, or dermatitis (especially eczema) in some individuals. Hence, one should keep this in mind when handling or using garlic. These toxic effects of garlic are due, to a large extent, to the sulfur-containing compounds present in garlic oil.

Traditional uses: The first recorded use of garlic in Chinese medicine dates back to the early 6th century. It has since been mentioned in most major herbals and is currently one of the official drugs listed in the pharmacopeia of the People's Republic of China.

According to Li Shizhen, garlic was introduced into China along with coriander about 2,000 years ago, during the Han Dynasty.

Garlic is considered to taste pungent, to be mildly toxic, and to have warming properties. It is said to act on and benefit the spleen, stomach, and lungs. Its most significant uses in Chinese medicine are as an antibiotic and anti-inflammatory agent in treating bacterial dysentery, amebic dysentery, enteritis (inflammation of the intestines), sores, carbuncles, and the common cold. Other conditions for which garlic is used include whooping cough, internal parasites, pulmonary tuberculosis, bellyache, nosebleeds, and snake and insect bites. The usual daily internal dose of garlic is 4.5 to 15 g. (0.16–0.5 oz.), taken as a decoction or eaten raw or cooked. Externally, it is usually mashed and applied directly to the affected areas.

Modern uses: During the past few decades, many clinical reports on garlic have appeared in Chinese national and regional medical or pharmaceutical journals. They have described the successful use of garlic and its preparations in treating numerous illnesses, including amebic and bacterial dysentery, pneumococcal pneumonia, whooping cough, diphtheria, icteric (jaundiced) infectious hepatitis, trachoma, suppurative middle-ear infection, hypersensitive teeth, candidiasis (a fungal infection), head ringworms, and acute appendicitis.

Allicin extracted from garlic is now available in China in capsule or injection form for treating bacterial and fungal infections. It is also used for lowering serum cholesterol and triglycerides for the prevention of atherosclerosis.

Home remedies: The northern Chinese use garlic quite often, but the southern Chinese seem to stay away from it because they don't like the odors it produces. I remember we used to envy the northerners' exceptional ability to resist colds, yet we used to joke about them, saying one could detect a northerner miles away by his garlic odor.

Certainly, there is no lack of remedies using garlic. The following are just a few of them.

For **nosebleed** that does not stop, a classical remedy calls for external use of garlic. After removing the membranous skin, one bulb of garlic is mashed to a paste, which is then formed into a patty the size and thickness of a U.S. silver dollar. This is taped on the middle of the right sole if the bleeding is from the right nostril, and on the left sole if from the left nostril. If bleeding is from both nostrils, then two garlic patties are used, one for each sole. It is said to produce fast relief, though there is no modern Chinese clinical report attesting to this claim.

To treat **diarrhea,** a 7th-century herbal recipe calls for simply taping mashed garlic on the middle of both soles or on one's navel.

Some Chinese households prepare a garlic wine and have it handy for the cold season. The wine is prepared by soaking three peeled garlic bulbs about 28 g. (1 oz.) each in 180 ml. (6 fl. oz.) of rice wine for at least one month. Then, when one catches a **cold,** one takes 15 ml. (about one tablespoonful) of this wine before retiring. To minimize the undesirable flavor, sugar dissolved in boiling water can be mixed in with the garlic wine immediately before taking it. It is said to be an effective remedy.

For treating painful **snakebites** and **insect bites,** a clove of crushed garlic is gently rubbed on the bitten area.

When a child has a **cough** that prevents him from sleeping at night, a clove of garlic is cut in half and the cut ends are rubbed gently on his throat. His cough then subsides and this allows him to sleep. Presumably this could apply to adults as well.

To treat **corns,** a modern remedy calls for use of garlic and green-onion bulbs. One bulb each of garlic and green onion are mashed together to a mudlike consistency. A small amount, enough to cover the corn, is applied and is secured by taping or wrapping. It is replaced by fresh material every two to three days. Some corns are removed after two applications. This remedy should not be used for more than four applications, and it should be discontinued if irritations develop.

Availability: Garlic is readily available in grocery stores and supermarkets.

GINGER

生姜

General information: Ginger has been used in both Eastern and Western folk medicine for centuries. Many Westerners who know about ginger probably first came across it by biting into it when eating in a Chinese restaurant and then wondering whether to spit it out or swallow it without further chewing. To the untrained palate, ginger is no fun to bite into. Even Chinese do not eat it much, except on special occasions. They use it mostly in small quantities as a condiment. The only time I have seen ginger eaten in any sizable amount is by women after childbirth to rebuild their strength.

What is commonly called ginger root is actually an underground stem. The plant is known scientifically as *Zingiber officinale* of the ginger family. In Chinese, fresh ginger is called *sheng jiang* and dried Chinese ginger is called *gan jiang.* It is a perennial herb with thick tuberous rhizomes (underground stems) from which the aerial stems rise to about 1 m. (3.3 ft.) tall. They bear relatively large leaves that are 15 to 30 cm. (6–12 in.) long and about 2 cm. (0.8 in.) wide. The cultivated ginger plant seldom flowers.

Ginger is believed to be native to the Pacific Islands. It is now widely cultivated in the tropics and in warm climates. Major ginger-producing countries include China, India, Jamaica, and Nigeria.

Both fresh and dried ginger roots are used in food and in medicine. But dried ginger is produced in much larger quantities; it is used for the preparation of ginger oil, extracts, and oleoresins. These are used widely in flavoring processed foods and soft drinks (e.g., ginger ale and ginger beer) as well as in cosmetic products such as perfumes (especially Oriental types and men's fragrances).

In Western folk medicine, ginger is mainly used as a carminative, appetite stimulant, and diaphoretic (promoting perspiration).

Many chemical constituents have been found in ginger. They include 1% to 3% volatile oil, pungent essences called gingerols, zingerone, and shogaols, about 9% protein, up to 50% starch, 6% to 8% fats, resins, minerals, vitamins (especially A and niacin), amino acids, and other biologically active chemicals. The volatile oil in turn contains dozens of chemical compounds and is responsible for the smell of ginger. Gingerols, zingerone, and shogaols are responsible for its biting, pungent taste.

A protein-digesting enzyme (protease) has recently been isolated from fresh ginger root in relatively high yield (2.26%). If further research is successful, ginger may some day turn up on your kitchen shelf as a meat tenderizer, which is now made mainly from papain from papaya.

Some Japanese studies have found ginger to contain strong antioxidants, which can keep potato chips, oily and fatty foods, and cookies from turning rancid or stale.

Effects on the body: Although much of the chemical research on ginger has been done in the West, most of the biological research has been done by Chinese and Japanese scientists. They have found that ginger has a wide variety of effects on microorganisms, animals, and humans. The best known is its ability to stop vomiting in experimental animals (e.g., dogs) and nausea and vomiting in humans. Shogaols are among its anti-emetic constituents. The carminative properties of ginger are also well known.

In experiments with rats previously fed cholesterol, scientists found that ginger extracts lowered the cholesterol levels in the blood and liver of these rats.

In one Chinese study, healthy human subjects were given 1 g. (0.04 oz.) of fresh ginger and told to chew it but not to swallow it. Their blood pressure was found to increase temporarily by an average of 11.2 mm. systolic and 14 mm. diastolic pressure.

Traditional uses: In Chinese medicine, ginger is used either fresh or dried. There is no problem for Westerners in identifying fresh ginger since it is the same fresh ginger root used in cooking. However, the dried ginger or powder on Western kitchen shelves is not the same as the dried ginger *(gan jiang)* used in Chinese medicine. For the latter, the rootstock from a different variety of the ginger plant is used. Hence the Western dried ginger spice should not be considered an equivalent of the Chinese dried ginger used medicinally.

The first recorded use of ginger in Chinese medicine dates back at least 2,000 years. It is described in the Shennong Herbal as being of medium quality, meaning that it could be toxic after long-term use. Traditionally, ginger (fresh or dried) is considered to have warming, diaphoretic, and antinausea and anti-emetic properties. It is also said to dissipate phlegm and stimulate the stomach and intestines. The more common medicinal uses of ginger include treatment of the common cold, nausea, vomiting, wheezing, coughing, nasal congestion, abdominal distention, diarrhea, and adverse effects of aconite and certain other drugs and foods (e.g., crabs and fish).

Perhaps the most widespread folk medicinal use of ginger, in the form of candied or preserved ginger, is in treating motion sickness. For this purpose, a small piece of ginger is chewed and eaten as often as necessary during a car or boat ride. I well remember when I was growing up in Hong Kong, our relatives visiting us from the villages used to come armed with preserved ginger and Tiger Balm or White Flower Oil. Buses used to reek of these medicines.

Although fresh ginger is sometimes used externally along with alum (potassium aluminum sulfate) to treat hemorrhoids and skin sores and boils, its long-term internal use is said to aggravate these conditions instead. Its use is also not recommended for pregnant women, even though they may experience nausea and vomiting.

The usual internal daily dose for both fresh and dried ginger is 3 to 9 g. (0.1–0.3 oz.). Fresh ginger is generally used in the form of expressed juice, a mash, or boiled in water. Dried ginger is usually used boiled in water.

Modern uses: The traditional uses of ginger described above have persisted for centuries. Other uses of ginger described in more modern herbals or Chinese medical or pharmaceutical journals include treatment of skin peeling from the hand, hemorrhoids, baldness, rheumatic pain, painful intestinal hernia, stomach and duodenal ulcers, malaria, acute bacillary dysentery, acute orchitis (inflammation of the testis), and drug poisoning (e.g., aconite and rhododendron). Some of these uses are reportedly quite effective, especially for malaria, rheumatic pain, and drug poisoning. The effectiveness of ginger in treating motion sickness has recently been confirmed in *The Lancet,* a well-known British medical journal.

Home remedies: Many remedies based on ginger are found in Chinese herbals, both classical and modern. The following are a few examples.

To treat **coughing, wheezing,** and **excessive phlegm** due to **colds,** a popular Cantonese remedy combines the use of ginger and black beans. A piece of fresh mature ginger, about 120 g. (4 oz.), is crushed with the flat side of a meat cleaver and placed in a hot frying pan with a small amount of black beans (30 g. or 1 oz.). The mixture is stir-fried until the ginger turns yellowish brown. Two cups of water are added and the mixture is boiled down to about one cup. The liquid, which is pungent, is drunk while hot before retiring. It will cause copious perspiration, and symptoms are said to disappear by the next day.

To treat **weakness after childbirth,** especially after a first child, fresh ginger is stewed with sweet vinegar, pig's feet, and whole eggs. The meat, eggs, ginger, and soup are all eaten, usually over a period of several weeks. Young ginger roots are generally selected for this purpose, because old roots are too pungent. This remedy is popular among Cantonese.

For treating long-term **unhealed sores** and **hemorrhoids,** ginger, with skin, is cut into large slices, covered with alum, and roasted dry. It is then ground into a fine powder and applied directly to the affected areas. This powder is also used to treat **toothache** by applying it directly on the aching tooth.

To treat **baldness,** a folk remedy from Guizhou calls for mashing fresh ginger, warming the mash, and spreading it directly on the bald area. Two to three applications are said to do the trick. I wonder.

Availability: Fresh ginger is sold in Chinese groceries and is also available in many Western supermarkets.

GINSENG

人参

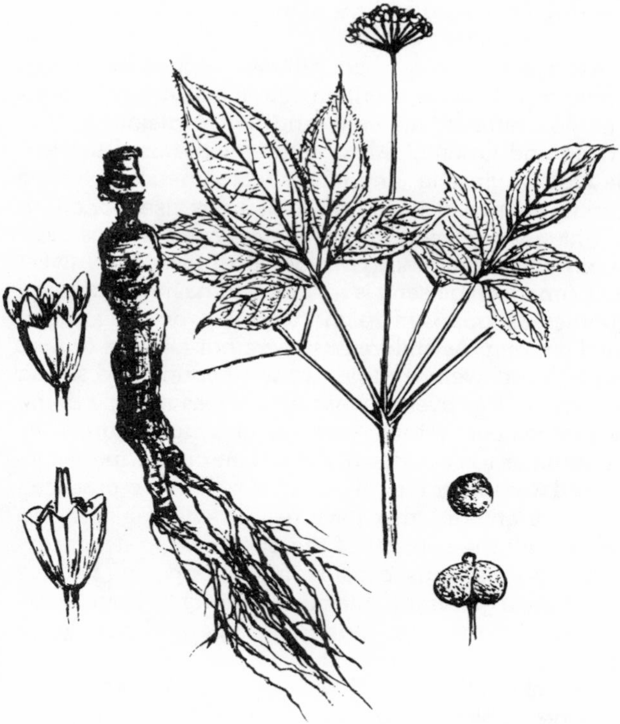

General information: Ginseng is probably the Chinese drug best known to Westerners. Many Western newspaper and magazine articles, as well as books, have been written on ginseng. It has also been the subject of jokes, especially about its alleged aphrodisiac properties. Despite its fame and all that is written about it, ginseng is still shrouded in mystery. Western advocates take it regularly and swear by it, but critics say that it is worthless and that its effects are all in the mind. In fact, only about 15 years ago, most of my American academic colleagues held this same opinion. But as more and more research data are coming out of Europe, Russia, China, Korea, and Japan, their view on ginseng has changed. Now they either believe that there must be something in ginseng that makes it work or are at least more open-minded about it.

Over the years, I have found two major problems relating to ginseng in America. The first concerns identifying it and its properties; the second, assessing its quality and the standards adhered to in its preparation.

Although sometimes well researched (but invariably based on English-language references) and well written, few, if any, of the writings on ginseng in English differentiate between the two major types of ginseng—American and Oriental. Most authors write as if the two were one single type of ginseng. The fact is that American ginseng and Oriental ginseng are two distinctly different drugs, used for different purposes in Chinese medicine. Few of their numerous uses overlap. Although both are traditionally considered to taste both sweet and slightly bitter, American ginseng is regarded as having cooling or even cold properties as opposed to the warming or invigorating nature of Oriental ginseng. As children we were not allowed to take Oriental ginseng because, we were told, we were young and strong and should not require it to overdo what nature was already doing for us. However, I remember we took American ginseng on numerous occasions in the summer to cool down. And when one of my sisters had scarlet fever and was under the care of a physician who practiced Western medicine, my grandmother gave her American ginseng to help cool her fever, with the consent of the doctor. My sister recovered with no complications. Thus, considering the opposing natures of American and Oriental ginseng, if one takes ginseng without knowing which type it is, one may use the wrong type and not derive benefits from its effects.

Even if one knows about the two different ginsengs and how to use them, one still has the problem of assessing the quality of the ginseng one buys and the standards used in its preparation. If one uses the actual root, at least one is sure that one will derive some real benefits, even if the grade of ginseng is not the best. But if one uses a prepared or powdered ginseng—in the form of a tablet, capsule, or liquid extract—one will not know what is really in it. Since there are no trade or government standards for ginseng preparations, a "ginseng" capsule, tablet, or extract may contain little or no ginseng at all, but, rather, diluents such as sugars and starches, with additives to give the product color or flavor (see also Aloe Vera). American consumers are spending a lot of money for sugar or starch pills, passed off as ginseng, many times overpriced, and some people are getting rich from this practice. If you want to use ginseng, stay away from bottled products, since, irrespective of manufacturers' claims or guaranties, at this time nobody can guarantee that they are genuine. Use only the root, which you can obtain from Chinese herb shops. These herb shops are run by professional herbalists, who genuinely serve the community. They are not out to make a quick financial killing, as are some of the people who make ginseng products in America. The chances of your buying an adulterated root or a substitute in a Chinese herb shop is certainly minute compared to your chances of getting cheated if you buy the bottled products manufactured by American companies from health food stores.

Oriental ginseng is scientifically called *Panax ginseng* or *Panax schinseng,* and American ginseng is called *Panax quinquefolius,* both of the ginseng family. Oriental ginseng is known in Chinese as *ren shen* ("man root"), and American ginseng is known as *xi yang shen*. It is also called Guangdong ginseng, referring to its original point of importation into China—Guangdong Province. Both are perennial herbs, with simple single stems bearing at flowering a whorl of three to six long-petioled compound leaves at the top. Oriental ginseng is a native of Manchuria and is extensively cultivated there and in nearby Siberia, Korea, and Japan. American ginseng is a native of North America and is cultivated throughout the United States (particularly in Wisconsin, West Virginia, Tennessee, North Carolina, and Missouri), and also in Canada (e.g., Quebec and Ontario).

The roots of both Oriental and American ginseng are harvested in early autumn. Normally plants six years or older are chosen. The roots are carefully dug up and washed carefully to avoid damaging them. After washing, they are dried under partial sunlight or low artificial heat (in the case of American ginseng), or subjected to further curing (washed, steamed, soaked in water, etc.) before drying (in the case of Orietal ginseng). There are many types and grades of Oriental ginseng, depending on the source, age, and part of the root and curing methods used. Wild, old, well-formed, undamaged roots are the most valued, while the rootlets of cultivated plants are considered of the lowest quality. Due to the fact that far fewer steps are involved in its processing, American ginseng has fewer grades.

Japanese and Russian scientists have done most of the research on the chemical composition of Oriental ginseng. They have found that it contains numerous saponins (foam-forming glycosides) that are believed to be its active constituents. The Japanese have named the ones they have identified ginsenosides, while the Russians have named theirs panaxosides. So far only one ginsenoside and one panaxoside have been found to be identical to one another. Oriental ginseng also contains highly variable amounts of starch (8%–32%), steroids (e.g., sitosterol), pectin, sugars, vitamins (e.g., B_1, B_2, B_{12}, nicotinic acid, pantothenic acid, and biotin), minerals (e.g., zinc, manganese, calcium, iron, and copper), choline, fats, and trace amounts of a volatile oil, among other constituents.

Research on American ginseng has been relatively limited. One major fact relating to its chemical constituents that is known is that American ginseng contains ginsenosides but no panaxosides. However, the relative proportions of ginsenosides in American ginseng are quite different from those in Oriental ginseng. Considering what are traditionally considered to be the different properties and uses of the two types of ginseng, it would not be surprising to find that, as more research unveils its other constituents, American ginseng differs from Oriental ginseng in other chemical aspects as well.

Effects on the body: Although hundreds of research papers on the effects of Oriental ginseng have been published over the past two or three decades by Chinese, Korean, Japanese, and Russian scientists, we still do not know how ginseng works. Its effects have been so numerous, so diversified, and sometimes so contradictory, that they must have frustrated some of the researchers. The effects of ginseng are generally believed to be due to its saponins, some of which produce effects directly opposed to those produced by others. Also, under certain conditions, depending on the state of the body, ginseng can act on it in completely contradictory ways.

Perhaps the word "adaptogen" can explain some of the actions of ginseng. This word has been coined only recently by Russian scientists and is not yet in our dictionaries. These scientists arrived at the "adaptogen theory" after observing the various effects of Oriental ginseng and other herbal tonics. An adaptogen, like ginseng, is defined as a substance that increases the body's resistance to outside stresses of various kinds, without causing it to deviate too much (if at all) from its normal functions. It achieves this effect by normalizing the physiological functions of the individual as a whole and not by acting on one specific part or function of the body. This sounds as if it has been taken directly out of a page of a book on the theory of Chinese medicine. The only difference is that the adaptogen theory is based on the results of scientific studies, while Chinese medicine has evolved over thousands of years through empirical observations.

Traditional uses: Oriental ginseng has been used medicinally in China for thousands of years. In the Shennong Herbal it is listed in the nontoxic category of herbs. Even at that time (ca. 200 B.C.), ginseng was considered to "vitalize the five organs, calm the nerves, stop palpitation due to fright, brighten vision, increase intellect, and, with long-term use, prolong life and make one feel young." After more than 2,000 years, the major properties and uses of Oriental ginseng are basically the same. Furthermore, the confidence and belief of the Chinese people in ginseng has not waned. If you are one of those who consider ginseng a joke, think twice before dismissing it as worthless. "Can billions of Chinese have been wrong for over two thousand years?"

In Chinese medicine, Oriental ginseng is considered a tonic and a sedative. It is also said to strengthen the heart and to promote body secretions. One of the official drugs listed in the pharmacopeia of the People's Republic of China, Oriental ginseng is used to treat various conditions that require strengthening the body's resistance. The major ones include mental or physical weakness or exhaustion resulting from a long-term illness, weak heart, asthma, palpitations, neurasthenia, spontaneous sweating, and cold limbs. Other conditions include amnesia, dizziness, headache, impotence, lack of appetite, nausea, and vomiting. The usual daily dose is 1.5 to 9 g. (0.05–0.3 oz.) taken as a decoction, powder, or pills—simply chewed in order to extract the juice.

American ginseng was introduced into China during the 18th century. At first it was thought to be identical to Oriental ginseng. But it was not long before the Chinese realized that its properties were different. Thus, according to an 18th-century herbal, American ginseng "tastes like ginseng but has cold properties, strengthens the *yin* and breaks fever." It is traditionally considered to benefit the lungs, dissipate heat, quench thirst, and promote body secretions. Although like Oriental ginseng it is considered a tonic, it is used under different bodily conditions: coughs, resulting from lung deficiencies, which are marked by short and shallow breath and dry throat, loss of blood, thirst, fever, irritability, tiredness, as well as toothache and hangover. None of the traditional records calls for its use as a general tonic. Rather, its use is primarily for treating conditions related to "heat" and "dryness." For this reason, American ginseng is very popular with southern Chinese (especially the Cantonese), who use it often in summer and for lowering fevers. The normal daily dose is 2.5 to 6 g. (0.09–0.2 oz.) taken as a decoction or chewed.

Oriental-ginseng leaf is considered to have qualities similar to those of American ginseng. It is used mainly for reducing fever or body heat in summer, quenching thirst, promoting body secretions, and treating hangovers.

As with other herbs, ginseng should not be brought in contact with metals (e.g., iron) during preparation.

Home remedies: Many remedies using Oriental ginseng for treating various illnesses can be found in traditional herbals; some of these date back many centuries, and most of them are complicated. Together with those handed down from generation to generation in Chinese families, these remedies, if collected, could fill a whole book. I have checked over four dozen recorded recipes and have not been able to find a single one that is simple enough to be presented here because most contain more than three herbs. It is understandable that ginseng is almost always prescribed with other herbs when it is used for treating specific conditions, since it is not meant to cure the illness by itself, but rather to strengthen the body and help the other herbs do their work. Hence, the following is a home remedy using Oriental ginseng only as a general tonic.

One of the traditional ginseng wines, for treating **neurasthenia, insomnia,** and **general weakness** after an illness, and for improving body strength and restoring virility, can be prepared in the following manner: Mix 100 g. (3.5 oz.) of finely chopped or thinly sliced ginseng with 1 liter (1 qt.) of a strong liquor together with an adequate amount of honey. Allow the mixture to stand in a dark, cool place for five to six weeks before it is ready for use. Leave the ginseng in the wine. When it is ready, each day after dinner or before retiring, drink 30 ml. (1 fl. oz.) of the wine. Rapidly increasing the daily dosage is said to cause more harm than good and is not recommended. This is probably one of the ginseng tonics known to Westerners as an aphrodisiac.

Although few recipes using American ginseng are recorded in traditional herbals, there is no lack of home remedies known to various Chinese families. The following is one of them.

A tea made from American ginseng is said to quench **thirst** due to hot weather and **sun exposure,** and at the same time relieve **tiredness.** To make this tea, steep one to two teaspoonfuls of American ginseng powder in a cup of boiling water for five to 10 minutes; then drink the tea.

Availability: Both Oriental and American ginseng roots are available whole, unground from Chinese herb shops. Better grades are considered more potent.

GREEN ONION

葱

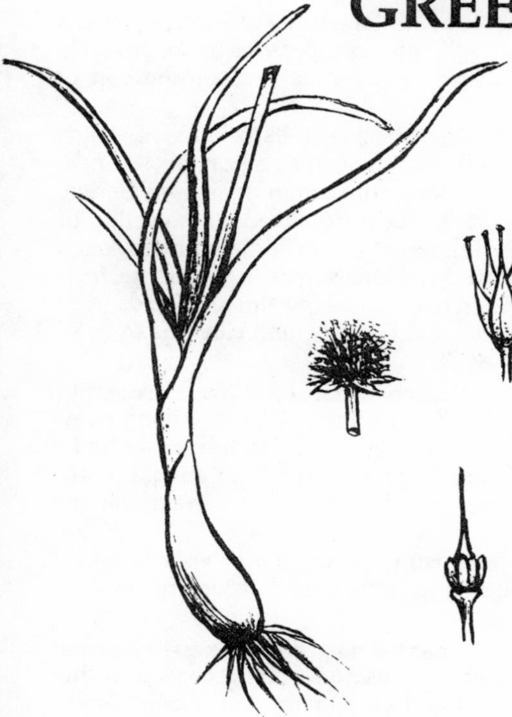

General information: Green onion is also known in English as scallion, spring onion, ciboule, Welsh onion, and Japanese bunching onion, and in Chinese as *cong.* Botanically, it is known as *Allium fistulosum* of the lily family. The Chinese name for the bulb, which is the part most commonly used medicinally, is *cong bai,* meaning "green onion white," a reference to its whitish color. The roots are called *cong xu,* "green onion beard." It is a perennial herb that can grow to about 50 cm. (20 in.) high and has green hollow leaves, about 1 to 1.5 cm. (0.4–0.6 in.) in diameter and pointed at the tip. Its bulb is cylindrical and not prominent, and is slightly thicker at the base. Green onion is a native of Asia but is now cultivated worldwide. It is relatively easy to grow from seed in any garden. However, in order for it to reach its full size, a warm climate and well-tended soil are required. In recent years, it has become common in many supermarkets. In Western households, it is more commonly used raw, as in salads. But in Chinese cooking, it is used raw and cooked with equal frequency, and it is a common ingredient in many Chinese dishes.

Unlike its relatives, garlic and onion, green onion is not traditionally used in Western folk medicine. In fact, it has gained popularity in Western cooking only during the past two decades or so, probably as a result of an increasing interest in Chinese food on the part of Westerners.

The pungent taste of green onion is due to its volatile oil, which consists of sulfur-containing compounds such as allicin, allyl sulfide, and dipropyl disulfide, similar to those present in garlic (see Garlic). In addition to alliin, from which allicin is produced by the action of the enzyme alliinase (see Garlic), green onion contains methylalliin and propylalliin. Other constituents include sugars (e.g., glucose, fructose, sucrose, and maltose), starch, cellulose, pectin, fatty acids (e.g., palmitic, stearic, oleic, arachidic, and linoleic), and vitamins (e.g., A, B_1, B_2, and C, and nicotinic acid).

Effects on the body: Many of the chemical constituents present in green onion, especially allicin and the other sulfur-containing compounds, have pharmacological properties similar to those present in garlic and onion (see Garlic), including antibacterial, antifungal, insecticidal, and can lower blood sugar and cholesterol levels in experimental animals and humans.

And since green onion contains the same type of volatile oil as does garlic, it can also cause skin irritations and blisters in sensitive individuals.

Traditional uses: Green onion has been used in Chinese medicine for thousands of years. Its medicinal use was first recorded in the Shennong Herbal, where it is listed among the herbs considered mildly toxic. All parts of the green-onion plant (leaves, bulb, flowers, seeds, roots, and juice) are used, but most usually the fresh bulb. Green onion is generally considered to taste pungent and to have warming properties.

Green-onion bulb is prepared by removing the green leaves above and roots below. What remains is a white bulb 2.5 to 5 cm (1–2 in.) long. It is said to promote perspiration, dissipate colds, restore vital functions of the body, and detoxify. Its best-known use is in treating the common cold and its associated symptoms, such as nasal congestion, runny nose, and headache. Other conditions for which green-onion bulb is used include bellyache, diarrhea, dysentery, carbuncles, kidney stones, earache, and difficulty in urinating. Traditionally, it should not be taken with honey. When used internally, its usual daily dose is 9 to 15 g. (0.3–0.5 oz.) boiled in water or wine. Externally, it is generally applied as a mash directly to the affected area.

Green-onion leaves are considered to have qualities similar to those of the bulb, and are used for treating the common cold and its symptoms, as well as stroke, painful sores and carbuncles, and traumatic injuries. The usual internal daily dose of green-onion leaves is 9 to 15 g. (0.3–0.5 oz.) boiled in water. Externally, they too are usually applied directly as a hot mash.

Green-onion roots are white, 2.5 to 5 cm. (1–2 in.) long, and, as their Chinese name suggests, do resemble a beard. These are the only parts of the green-onion plant that are not considered to have warming properties. Green-onion roots are used to treat headache due to the common cold, injuries due to excessive cold (e.g., frostbite), and sores in the throat. The daily internal dose is usually 6 to 9 g. (0.2–0.3 oz.) taken as a decoction. Externally, either the powdered dried roots are applied directly or a decoction is used for washing the affected areas.

Green-onion seeds are considered to invigorate kidney functions and brighten vision. They are used for treating impotence due to kidney deficiencies, dizziness, seminal emission, and white vaginal discharge. Their usual daily dose is 3 to 9 g. (0.1–0.3 oz.) taken as a powder with water.

Green-onion juice, obtained from the bulb or the whole plant is considered to have the ability to disperse blood stasis (e.g., clotting, black and blue marks), detoxify, and expel internal parasites. It is used for treating headache, nosebleeds, hematuria (bloody urine), internal parasites, carbuncles, and traumatic injuries.

Modern uses: Successful uses of green-onion bulb, based on traditional remedies, have been reported in numerous Chinese regional pharmaceutical and medical journals for treatment of the common cold, mastitis, indigestion in children, and pinworms. In all cases, it was combined with other herbs.

The external use of green-onion bulb in the treatment of the common cold has been described in a Japanese report. A mixture of 15 g. (0.5 oz.) each of green-onion bulb and fresh ginger was mashed with 3 g. (0.1 oz.) of salt. The resulting mash was wrapped in gauze and used to rub the chest, back, soles, palms, bends of the elbows, and the hollow at the back of the knees. After being rubbed, the patient was allowed to lie down to rest. All 107 patients with colds treated by this method recovered in one to two days. Most required only one treatment and recovered overnight. A few needed two treatments and were well in two days. In some patients, fever disappeared half an hour after the first rubbing with the herbal mash, during which they perspired copiously.

Home remedies: Many recipes based on green onion exist in Chinese herbals, both classical and modern. A few examples follow.

To treat the **common cold** and resultant **headache,** a typical recipe (see also Bean Curd) calls for boiling 31 to 62 g. (1.1–2.2 oz.) of green-onion bulb (with roots) and 15 g. (0.5 g.) of fresh ginger in water for about 20 to 30 minutes. After decanting or straining, the liquid is drunk before retiring.

For an **itchy throat with nasal congestion and an urge to cough,** a noodle soup can be prepared with a few green-onion bulbs and one or two pieces of fresh ginger the size of a U.S. quarter. A pinch of white pepper is sprinkled in and the whole mixture is eaten hot.

For **kidney stones,** stew 225 g. (0.5 lb.) each of whole green onion and pig's feet in an adequate amount of water. No salt should be added. The whole mixture is then eaten. It certainly doesn't hurt to try this remedy if one can stomach pig's feet.

To treat **seminal emission** or **white vaginal discharge,** a recipe in a modern practical herbal calls for taking 3 g. (0.1 oz.) dried, ground green-onion seeds, two to three times daily, with water. A total dose of 93 g. (3.3 oz.) may be taken over a period of 10 days.

To treat **indigestion** in children, a remedy consisting of one whole green onion, 15 g. (0.5 oz.) of fresh ginger, and 9 g. (0.3 oz.) of powdered fennel seed is used. The green onion and ginger are finely mashed. The powdered fennel seed is added, and the whole mash is mixed well. It is then heated to the point where it is hot but bearable when placed on the skin, then wrapped in gauze and placed on the child's navel. This can be done once or twice daily for several days.

For treating **traumatic injuries** and painful, **bleeding wounds** such as **finger injuries,** a remedy that appears in several classical herbals calls for the use of green-onion leaves. The fresh leaves are heated up slowly until hot, then split open and the inner side (now slimy) is placed directly on the wound with slight pressure. This process is repeated with fresh hot leaves until pain and bleeding subside. According to Li Shizhen, the 16th-century herbalist, several applications will work, and the wound will heal with no scars.

Hua Tuo, a famous surgeon of the 3d century A.D. who is credited with perfecting the art of acupunture, has described a remedy for treating sudden **exhaustion** in men due to **excessive sexual intercourse,** resulting in **cold perspiration** and **unconsciousness.** According to his recipe, green-onion bulbs are stir-fried until hot (but not burning) and placed on the man's navel. In the meantime, several green-onion bulbs are mashed and cooked in wine, which is then fed to the patient. This remedy is said to restore the patient's *yang qi* (male vitality).

Availability: Green onions are sold in most supermarkets and some grocery stores. Green-onion seeds are available in Chinese herb shops.

HONEY

蜜糖

General information: Honey has been with us for thousands of years. There is scarcely anyone who has not tasted it. It is produced worldwide and comes in different colors (pale yellowish to reddish brown) and textures (thin to relatively thick). Honey is a favorite source of sugar for health food enthusiasts. Since it has been used in Western folk medicine for centuries, there is no lack of Western home remedies based on honey. It is produced by certain kinds of honeybees, notably *Apis mellifera* and *Apis cerana.* The composition and flavor of honey vary depending on the type of bee, its food source and environment. Usually about 70% to 80% of honey is made up of fructose and glucose. The remaining constituents include other sugars (e.g., sucrose and maltose), proteins, organic acids, enzymes, small amounts of minerals, and numerous vitamins. One hundred grams (3.3 oz.) of honey supplies about 300 calories.

Traditional uses: Honey in Chinese is called *mi tang.* It is described in the Shennong Herbal and *Ben Cao Gang Mu* and in most other major Chinese herbals. Hence, its recorded use in Chinese medicine dates back at least 2,000 years. It is considered to have soothing, pain-killing, detoxifying and mildly laxative properties. Some of its more common uses include the treatment of cough, chronic bronchitis, constipation, stomachache, nasal sinus conditions (with nasal congestion, smelly nasal discharge, dizziness, and blurred vision), canker sores, thermal burns, and aconite poisoning.

Modern uses: In recent years, the effectiveness of some of the traditional uses of honey has been documented in Chinese and Japanese medical journals. These uses include the treatment of ulcers of the stomach and duodenum, thermal burns, chilblains, hard-to-heal chronic skin ulcers, minor wounds, dermatitis, eczema, rhinitis, and inflammation of the nasal sinuses.

In both a Chinese and a Japanese report on the successful treatment of stomach and duodenal ulcers, over 82% of several hundred patients treated were cured. The patients were given fresh honey (33 g., or 1.2 oz.) three times daily before meals. After 10 days, the dose was increased one-and-a-half to two times the initial dosage. Although the pain of some of the patients who responded to this treatment disappeared in as little as six days, it usually took a few weeks for this treatment to take effect.

Several Chinese and Japanese reports have also described the successful use of honey in the topical treatment of thermal burns, especially first- and second-degree burns. In this treatment, honey was spread on a piece of clean cloth, which was then placed directly on the cleaned, burned area. This was done a few times daily until a scab was formed; the honey application was then reduced to one or two times daily. Of the 85 patients treated by this method, most generally formed a transparent scab two to three days after treatment started. This scab peeled off by itself, usually on the sixth to tenth day, leaving completely newly formed skin. This treatment was reported to be effective even with patients who were admitted to the hospital late and whose wounds had already been infected.

Home remedies: As in Western folk medicine, there are many Chinese home remedies using honey. For example, to treat **dry stool** or **constipation,** two tablespoonfuls of honey are dissolved in a glass of boiled water and drunk once daily. This is said to be particularly good for habitual constipation in older people.

To treat **dry cough** or **dry throat,** one tablespoonful of honey is dissolved in a glass of boiled water and taken twice daily.

For treating **white hair** in young people, an old remedy calls for pulling off the white hairs and then rubbing the empty hair follicles with a small amount of honey. The hair is said to grow out to its original dark color.

For **minor burns,** such as those caused by splattering hot oil during cooking, simply apply a small amount of honey directly to the burned area.

To treat **ulcers** of the stomach or duodenum, 56 g. (2 oz.) of honey is used with 9 g. (0.3 oz.) of licorice and 6 g. (0.2 oz.) of tangerine peel. The licorice and tangerine peel are first boiled together in water. After straining or decanting to remove the residue, the honey is dissolved in the remaining liquid, which is then drunk in three separate portions during the day.

A recipe for treating both **high blood pressure** and chronic **constipation** calls for 56 g. (2 oz.) of honey and 47 g. (1.7 oz.) of black sesame seeds. The sesame seeds are cooked by steaming and then mashed. The honey is added to the mash and the whole mixture is divided into two portions, one to be taken in the morning and the other at night. Before the mixture is taken, it is dissolved in hot water that has been boiled.

Availability: Honey of various origins is widely available in supermarkets, groceries, and health food stores. Chinese honey can be bought in Chinese groceries.

HONEYSUCKLE

金銀花

General information: Honeysuckle is a collective name for numerous twining or trailing shrubs with opposite leaves and mildly fragrant to very fragrant flowers. These plants are known scientifically as *Lonicera* of the honeysuckle family. The Japanese honeysuckle *(Lonicera japonica)* is the honeysuckle most commonly used in Chinese medicine, but several other species are also used.

In Chinese, honeysuckle flowers are called *jin yin hua,* meaning, literally, "gold and silver flowers." The term refers to the color of the flowers of Japanese honeysuckle, which are at first white but then change to golden yellow. Honeysuckle stems or vines are called *ren dong teng,* meaning "winter-resistant vine," which refers to the hardy nature of the vines.

Japanese honeysuckle is a native of Asia but now grows wild in many parts of North America, especially the northeastern United States. Its climbing or twining stem can reach as much as 9 m. (30 ft.) long. Its flowers are very fragrant.

Honeysuckle is not a popular folk medicine in Western countries, but it is widely used in traditional Chinese medicine. Thus, it comes as no surprise that most of the chemical, biological, pharmacological, and clinical research that has been published on honeysuckle has been done by Chinese researchers. These researchers have found Japanese honeysuckle stems, leaves, and flowers to contain numerous constituents, including luteolin, luteolin derivatives (e.g., lonicerin), alkaloids, tannins, inositol, loganin, secologanin, chlorogenic acid, and saponins. Chlorogenic acid is believed to be the major active constituent. Among the commonly used honeysuckle species, including *Lonicera confusa, L. hypoglauca,* and *L. dasystyla,* chlorogenic acid content ranges from less than 0.5% to almost 7%.

The flowers and the stems, with leaves, of the honeysuckle plant are commonly used in Chinese medicine and are produced throughout China.

Honeysuckle flowers are collected during May or June (the flowering season in China is May to July). Traditionally picked in the morning after the dew has evaporated, they are laid out in thin layers on straw mats and are sun-dried or air-dried in the shade. Harsh midday and early afternoon sun is avoided. The flowers are turned over occasionally to insure even drying.

Honeysuckle stems (or vines) with leaves are collected in autumn or winter. They are tied in small bundles and sun-dried.

Effects on the body: Luteolin, a principal constituent of honeysuckle, is muscle-relaxant, mildly diuretic, and antibacterial, and extracts of Japanese honeysuckle have been found to have strong antibacterial effects on a wide variety of bacteria.

When Chinese scientists gave an extract of Japanese honeysuckle flowers to rats on a high cholesterol diet, they found that the rats' blood cholesterol level became lower than that in rats not on a high cholesterol diet. They believe that honeysuckle flower extract can retard the absorption of cholesterol from the intestines, resulting in less cholesterol in the blood.

Recently, in China, an extract of Japanese honeysuckle containing isochlorogenic and chlorogenic acids as its major active ingredients was found to be effective in treating acute laryngitis, acute pharyngitis, excess menstruation, uterine bleeding, and skin abscesses.

Japanese scientists have also found hot-water extracts of Japanese honeysuckle to prevent stomach ulcers in experiments with rats.

In papers that appeared in 1982 in Western scientific journals *(Proceedings of the National Academy of Sciences of the United States* and *Carcinogenesis*), American and French researchers reported chlorogenic acid to protect against substances that cause cancer in experimental animals and to prevent the formation of carcinogens, such as nitrosamines from nitrites.

Traditional uses: Honeysuckle has been used in Chinese medicine for thousands of years. Its first recorded medicinal use is in the Shennong Herbal, and it has since been described in all major Chinese herbals.

Honeysuckle flowers and stems with leaves possess similar therapeutic properties. The most important and well-known are their abilities to dissipate heat (or fever), to reduce inflammation, and to detoxify. They are used in treating fever, influenza, sore throat, mumps, bacterial dysentery, enteritis, acute laryngitis, skin sores, boils, erysipelas (a skin disease), acute mastitis, swollen and painful joints, infections and inflammation of the bile ducts, rheumatism, and other conditions. Both herbs are currently official drugs in China and are listed in the pharmacopeia of the People's Republic of China.

The usual internal dose for honeysuckle flowers is 6 to 15 g. (0.2–0.5 oz.) and that for honeysuckle stems or vines is 9 to 30 g. (0.3–1 oz.). They are usually boiled in water and the decoction taken. Occasionally, the herbs are left in wine for a period of weeks or months and the resulting extraction is drunk as a tonic. The powdered herbs can also be taken directly.

For external applications, a decoction is used to wash affected areas (e.g., for boils and sores) or the powdered herbs are applied directly as a wet mash.

Together with other detoxifying herbs (notably dandelion, licorice, and chrysanthemum flowers) honeysuckle is often used for what Chinese medicine calls "toxic" conditions, such as swellings, sores, and boils.

Modern uses: Due to the fact that honeysuckle has a long history of use and is well known for its anti-inflammatory, antipyretic, and detoxifying properties, as well as because of its nontoxic nature, considerable efforts have been made in China during the past few decades to bring its use into modern clinical settings. Numerous reports on its clinical uses and effectiveness have appeared in national and regional medical journals, journals of traditional Chinese medicine, and research journals. Successful modern uses include treatment of laryngitis, pharyngitis, pneumonia, pulmonary tuberculosis, respiratory tract infections, acute bacterial dysentery, infantile diarrhea, surgical infections, conjunctivitis, infectious hepatitis, appendicitis, and enteritis. As in traditional medicine, most of the modern treatments call for honeysuckle in combination with various other herbal drugs. Honeysuckle flowers are also one of the numerous components in the formulation of treatments of cancers (e.g., angiosarcoma and cancers of the tonsil, bladder, and colon).

The following examples of modern uses reported for honeysuckle do not call for complicated herbal combinations.

A combination of honeysuckle flowers and whole dandelion herb was used for treating inflammatory eye diseases (conjunctivitis, keratitis, and corneal ulcer). A solution for use as eye drops was prepared from 63 g. (2.2 oz.) each of honeysuckle flowers and dandelion to make 1,000 ml. (33.8 fl. oz.). The solution was applied hourly to the eyes, two to three drops at a time, until the eye conditions healed. The treatment took three to seven days, with acute eye diseases yielding the best results.

For treating infectious hepatitis, 63 g. (2.2 oz.) of honeysuckle vines were boiled in 1,000 ml. (33.8 fl. oz.) of water until this was reduced to 400 ml. (13.5 fl. oz.). The decoction was taken in two equal doses, one in the morning and one at night. This daily treatment lasted 15 days. Of 22 patients thus treated, 12 had no more symptoms, and their liver functions had returned to normal by the end of the treatment, while six patients simply improved and four did not respond.

Home remedies: Many remedies calling for honeysuckle are recorded in traditional herbals as well as in modern popular drug manuals. Only a small proportion of these contain honeysuckle alone or in simple combinations. The following are a few examples.

To treat infected **skin boils and sores,** or acute **pharyngitis,** a recipe in a popular modern practical herbal calls for honeysuckle flowers combined with two other well-known detoxifying herbs. Honeysuckle flowers (15 g., or 0.5 oz.) are mixed with wild chrysanthemum flowers (9 g., or 0.3 oz.) and licorice (6 g., or 0.2 oz.) and boiled in about three cups of water down to one and a half cups or one cup. After its is strained or decanted off, the resulting liquid is drunk.

For treating **influenza** with fever, thirst, and aching body, 31 g. (1.1 oz.) of honeysuckle vines with leaves (triple the quantity if fresh) is boiled in water and drunk as a tea.

To treat **mushroom poisoning,** a modern herbal gives the following remedy: Wash fresh young honeysuckle stems and leaves in water that has been boiled and allowed to cool. Chew the stems and leaves well and swallow.

To treat **laryngitis** or **pharyngitis,** a decoction prepared by boiling 15 g. (0.5 oz.) of honeysuckle flowers and 3 g. (0.1 oz.) of licorice in water is used as a gargle. This liquid is reported to reduce inflammation and swelling and to speed up the healing process.

When I was growing up in Hong Kong, honeysuckle was to my family what aspirin is to an American family. We used honeysuckle flowers for **fevers** and **colds** quite often. For these conditions, 6 to 15 g. (0.2–0.5 oz.) of honeysuckle flowers are boiled in about 1 liter (1 qt.) of water down to about one-third the volume. The liquid is strained or decanted off and drunk. For children, the dose is reduced.

Availability: Honeysuckle flowers and stems or vines with leaves are available from Chinese herb shops. Fresh honeysuckle is readily found in fields and yards throughout North America and Europe.

LICORICE

甘草

General information: Perhaps the most frequently prescribed herb in Chinese medicine, licorice (or liquorice) is no stranger to Westerners. It has been used medicinally in Western cultures for several thousand years. Most Westerners probably know it as the flavor in the popular licorice candy, though few realize that this "licorice flavor" is actually anise rather than licorice (see Star Anise). The fact is that licorice has hardly any smell but tastes pleasantly sweetish, while anise smells and tastes strongly aromatic.

Also known as sweet wood and glycyrrhiza (especially in pharmaceutical usage), licorice consists of the dried underground stems (runners) and roots of several plants of the pea family, including *Glycyrrhiza uralensis, Glycyrrhiza glabra, Glycyrrhiza inflata,* and *Glycyrrhiza kansuensis.* Among these, *Glycyrrhiza uralensis* is the most commonly used in Chinese medicine. In Chinese, licorice is called *gan cao,* meaning "sweet herb."

Licorice plants are perennial herbs or subshrubs, generally with long horizontal underground stems and long taproots (main roots). The erect stem rises from 0.3 m. to 2 m. (1–6.5 ft.) above the ground.

Licorice is generally considered to be a native of Eurasia and is now cultivated in many parts of the world, especially Europe (e.g., Spain, Italy, England, and France), the Middle East (e.g., Iran, Iraq, Syria, and Turkey), Russia, and Asia (particularly China).

Licorice roots (including runners) are collected in the spring and fall. They are cut into sections, usually 30 to 120 cm. (1–4 ft.) long and dried under the sun until they are half-dried. They are then tied into bundles and left further under the sun until completely dry. Some types of licorice roots are peeled. In the West, much of the licorice used is in the form of extracts, which usually come dried as sticks or blocks. They are produced by steeping licorice roots in hot water, evaporating off the water, and then drying the extracts to form the sticks or blocks.

Licorice is one of the most researched medicinal herbs in modern times. Over the past several decades, more than a thousand scientific reports on licorice have appeared throughout the world. Due to the efforts of scientists we now know that licorice is made up of over 150 chemical compounds. Its major active principle is glycyrrhizin, which is also known as glycyrrhizic or glycyrrhizinic acid. Glycyrrhizin is present in licorice in highly variable amounts (1%–24%). It tastes 50 times sweeter than sucrose (cane sugar); when mixed with sucrose or other sugars it tastes even sweeter.

Licorice also contains highly variable amounts of starch (2%–20%) and sugars (3%–14%), depending on the source, as well as many types of biologically active compounds such as steroids, flavonoids, amines, and triterpenoids.

In Western folk medicine, licorice is considered a demulcent, expectorant, wound-healer, mild laxative, diuretic, and thirst-quencher. It has been used for several thousand years to treat ulcers, diseases of the bladder and kidney, laryngitis, sore throat, coughs, asthma, tuberculosis, fevers, rheumatism, and various other ailments. Extracts of licorice are widely used as ingredients in cough drops and syrups, laxatives, tonics, diuretics, antismoking lozenges, and other over-the-counter preparations. They are also used as flavoring agents to mask bitter, nauseous, or other undesirable tastes in certain otherwise unpalatable medicines (e.g., aloe, cascara, ammonium chloride, and quinine preparations).

Licorice is also used extensively in processed foods and beverages, especially licorice candy, where it is combined with star anise oil.

Effects on the body: Like ginseng, licorice is an herb that has many different effects on the body. The following effects of licorice have been verified by modern scientific research: It reduces blood cholesterol, fevers, and inflammation; promotes wound healing; increases bile secretion; decreases gastric secretion; increases blood sodium but decreases blood potassium; and promotes estrus. Licorice has also been shown to be antitussive, anticonvulsive, anti-ulcer, antibacterial, anti-allergic, and to inhibit the growth of experimentally induced tumors. Many of these biological effects have been found to be due to glycyrrhizin, but others cannot be explained.

During the past few decades, the effects of licorice on the adrenal glands have been well studied. It was observed that people who consumed excessive amounts of licorice candy (over 113 g., or 4 oz., daily) and patients with peptic ulcers who took anti-ulcer licorice preparations for an extended period of time, developed symptoms that included edema, weight gain, high blood pressure, and abnormal heart functions. Based on these observations, scientists fed licorice candy to healthy volunteers and found that as little as 100 g. (3.5 oz.) of licorice candy daily produced the above symptoms in one to four weeks. There was pronounced sodium retention and potassium excretion, resulting in hypokalemia (low serum potassium). However, these effects were not permanent; the symptoms disappeared after the subjects stopped taking licorice. Nevertheless, one should be reminded not to indulge in licorice candy or other licorice-based products, especially if one is overweight or has hypertension, or kidney or heart problems.

Traditional uses: Said to have first been used by the emperor Shennong some 5,000 years ago, licorice is probably the most widely used herb in Chinese medicine. Its first recorded use in Chinese medicine appeared in the Shennong Herbal, where it is listed in the nontoxic category of herbs.

Although licorice is used specifically for treating various illnesses, its most frequent use by far is as a complementary herb in countless herbal prescriptions. Its main function in these prescriptions is either to bring out the best beneficial effects of other herbs or to moderate their toxic effects.

In Chinese medicine, licorice is considered to have essentially the same therapeutic properties as in Western folk medicine. It is also used to treat many of the same types of conditions. There are major differences, however, especially in the emphasis placed on licorice and the frequency of use in treating various conditions. Thus, in Chinese medicine, licorice is most often used to treat sore throat, cough, palpitations (heart pounding), stomachache or nervous stomach, ulcers of the digestive tract, and sores. Another important and frequent use of licorice (apparently not practiced in Western folk medicine) is in treating drug or food poisoning. Even in these specific applications, licorice is seldom used by itself, but rather along with other herbs. The usual daily dose is 1.5 to 15 g. (0.05–0.5 oz.). For the treatment of poisoning, a single dose can be as much as 31 g. (1.1

oz.). Internally, licorice is normally taken as a decoction, powder, or pills. For external use, it is soaked or boiled in water and the liquid used for washing affected areas.

Modern uses: In recent years, many of the traditional uses of licorice have been tested in China under modern clinical settings, and their effectiveness has been verified by modern clinical methods. Dozens of reports on its effectiveness have appeared in Chinese national and regional, as well as some Japanese, journals of medicine and science.

The best-documented modern clinical use of licorice is in the treatment of peptic ulcers, for which it is 90% effective. Patients are generally given daily doses of 7.5 to 15 g. (0.26–0.5 oz.) of licorice root for one to two weeks. A longer course of treatment, up to six weeks, is sometimes adopted, but at the risk of patients developing high blood pressure, edema, and cardiac asthma. Licorice is more effective when taken in its crude powdered form than in its extracted form (e.g., decoction or commercial extracts), since the crude form retains all its active ingredients while the extracted forms have lost some of these during the extraction process.

Other effective uses of licorice that have been scientifically documented include treatments of Addison's disease (marked by extreme weakness, weight loss, low blood pressure, gastrointestinal disturbance, and brownish pigmentation of the skin and mucous membranes), tuberculosis, chronic bronchial asthma, diabetes insipidus, frostbite, infectious hepatitis, thrombophlebitis (inflammation of a vein with the formation of a blood clot), dermatitis, and acute schistosomiasis (a visceral disease caused by parasites).

Home remedies: Licorice is seldom used alone, but the following remedies are examples of the few instances in which it is used either alone or in combination with only one or two other herbs.

To treat **stomach ulcer** or **duodenal ulcer,** a decoction of licorice alone is used. The decoction is prepared by boiling 15 g. (0.5 oz.) of licorice in three cups of water for about 30 minutes, until one to one-and-a-half cups remain. This liquid is taken once daily for one to two weeks.

To treat **sore throat,** a decoction of licorice is prepared similarly with 12 g. (0.4 oz.) of licorice, and is taken once daily for one to three days.

To treat **stomachache, bellyache,** or **vomiting** due to virus infection, a decoction of 12 g. (0.4 oz.) of licorice and 6 g. (0.2 oz.) of ginger is used.

If one has accidentally ingested an unknown **poison** which cannot be treated with a specific antidote, a decoction of 31 g. (1.1 oz.) each of licorice and black soybeans or mung beans (see Soybean and Mung Beans) can be used.

To treat **lead poisoning,** a modern recipe calls for boiling 9 g. (0.3 oz.) of licorice with 12 g. (0.4 oz.) of almonds (with skin and tips removed) in about four cups of water until they are reduced to about one-and-a-half cups (30 to 40 minutes). This decoction is taken twice a day for three to five days.

For **insomnia, anxiety,** and **palpitations,** boil 3 g. (0.1 oz.) of licorice with 3 g. (0.1 oz.) of *shi chang pu (Acorus gramineus)* in two to three cups of water for 30 to 40 minutes until one-third to one-half of the liquid remains. After decanting or straining, the liquid is divided into two equal portions and one is taken in the morning and one at night.

A versatile preparation that doubles as a condiment and a salve for kitchen **burns** can be prepared by soaking 15 g. (0.5 oz.) of licorice (sliced) in two cups of hot honey for two hours. After straining while still warm, the licorice honey is ready for later use.

Availability: Crude licorice sticks and slices are available from health food stores and from Chinese herb shops.

LUFFA

丝瓜

General information: Luffa, or loofah, is also known as vegetable sponge or dishcloth gourd. It is the fibrous remains of the old mature fruit of *Luffa cylindrica* of the gourd family. It is commonly used as a sponge for bathing or dishwashing. Its Chinese name is *si gua luo.*

The plant is an annual vine, native to tropical Asia. It is hairy when young but turns practically hairless as it matures. Its stem can reach as much as 10 m. (33 ft.) long. Its mature yellow fruit is usually 30 to 60 cm. (1–2 ft.) long, cylindrical, and often slightly curved. The young green fruit is a popular vegetable among Cantonese, particularly in soups.

The fruit is allowed to grow old and is harvested in autumn, usually after the first frost. The pulp, skin, and seeds are then removed by rubbing. Alternatively, the fruit is soaked in water until the skin and pulp become rotten; these are then washed off along with the seeds and the spongelike luffa is sun-dried. In its final form, luffa has a tough, wiry, resilient texture. Its diameter is 6 to 10 cm. (2.5–4.0 in.). Luffa is produced mainly in southeastern China, especially in the provinces of Jiangsu, Guangdong, and Zhejiang.

Luffa is no stranger to beauty-conscious Westerners. For years they have used it as a body sponge to remove dead skin tissue and to stimulate the skin. It is tough enough for efficient skin cleansing yet not abrasive enough to damage the skin if used wet and with moderation.

Traditional uses: Luffa has been used in Chinese medicine since the 10th century. It is described in Li Shizhen's *Ben Cao Gang Mu* and is currently listed in the pharmacopeia of the People's Republic of China. Luffa is said to promote blood circulation, facilitate energy flow in the body, dissipate fever, and break up phlegm. It is used to treat aching body and limbs, tight chest, backache, bellyache, swollen and painful testicles, amenorrhea, hemorrhoids, intestinal and uterine hemorrhages, and inadequate milk flow in nursing mothers. It is generally boiled in water and the resulting decoction taken internally. The usual daily dose is 5 to 10 g. (0.17–0.35 oz.). For external use, luffa is gently heated in a sealed vessel for several hours until it is completely charred; the powdered charcoal is directly applied to the affected areas.

Modern uses: In 1982 a report in the *Chinese Journal of Ophthalmology* described the use of luffa charcoal in treating three patients with shingles (*herpes zoster*) in the face and eye region. The powdered charcoal was mixed with 50% alcohol to form a paste, which was painted directly on the rash. All three patients were in severe pain, which two of them had experienced for three days; treatment with modern painkilling drugs had not brought relief. Repeated application of luffa charcoal paste completely relieved the pain, absorbed the vesicles (blisters), and started the healing process after two days of use. No other types of medication were given along with luffa. All three patients completely recovered five to seven days after the luffa treatment started.

Home remedies: To treat **sprained back** or **arthritic pain,** 15 g. (0.5 oz.) of luffa is cut up and boiled gently in water down to one-third or one-quarter of its volume. The resulting decoction is strained or decanted off and taken once daily mixed with a small amount of white wine.

Availability: Luffa usually comes in cut pieces, 10 to 20 cm. (4–8 in.) long. It is available in health food stores and Chinese grocery stores.

MARIGOLD

万寿菊

General information: Two species of marigold are used in Chinese medicine—the big, or Aztec, marigold and the French marigold. Big, or Aztec, marigold is known scientifically as *Tagetes erecta* and French marigold as *Tagetes patula,* both of the composite family. In Chinese, Aztec marigold is called *wan shou ju,* meaning "long-life chrysanthemum," and French marigold is known as *xi fan ju,* meaning "Western chrysanthemum," denoting its foreign origin. The whole French marigold plant, when used in traditional medicine, is called *kong que cao,* or "peacock herb."

Marigolds are strong-scented annual herbs, usually 0.3 to 1 m. (1–3 ft.) tall. Aztec marigold bears flower heads that range in color from yellow to orange and can reach as much as 10 cm. (4 in.) across, while French marigold bears yellow to golden-yellow flower heads that are much smaller, only up to about 4 cm. (1.6 in.) across and usually with red patches. Both marigolds are generally considered to be natives of Mexico. They are now extensively cultivated throughout the world, with numerous varieties.

Although both marigolds are commonly seen as ornamental plants in Western countries, Aztec marigold is quite extensively grown for its yellow flower heads. The flower petals are used in chicken feed to give the skin and egg yolk of chickens the familiar yellow color. This practice has been going on for so many years, and Western consumers have grown so used to the yellow color of chicken skin and egg yolk, that most of them believe this color to be natural and actually consider chickens without a yellow skin and eggs without yellow yolks unnatural and undesirable. Marigolds also yield a fragrant volatile oil called tagetes oil that is used in perfumes and in many types of processed food products, including alcoholic and nonalcoholic beverages, frozen desserts, candies, puddings, condiments, and relishes.

In Western folk medicine, the flower heads and leaves of Aztec marigold are used in treating intestinal worms and colic, as well as in promoting menstrual flow.

Effects on the body: Scientists have found tagetes oil to have various effects on experimental animals. These include sedative, anticonvulsive, hypotensive, bronchodilatory, and anti-inflammatory effects. Tagetes oil also has insecticidal properties.

As is typical in plants of the composite family, marigolds can cause contact dermatitis in some sensitive individuals. Consequently, if one is allergic to chrysanthemums, daisies, or other composite plants one should be careful about handling marigolds also.

Traditional uses: The uses of marigolds in Chinese medicine are described only in modern herbals that are mainly of southern Chinese origin. Despite this lack of written record, marigolds have probably been used for generations as a folk remedy in some southern Chinese provinces, particularly Yunnan, Guizhou, Sichuan, and Guangxi. Both the flower heads and leaves of Aztec marigold are usually collected in the summer or fall and are used either fresh or sun-dried.

The flower heads of Aztec marigold are considered to have properties that dissipate heat (in fevers), expel colds, and break up phlegm. They are used to treat whooping cough, coughs due to colds, convulsions in children, acute conjunctivitis, dizziness, mumps, and mastitis. The usual daily internal dose is 3 to 9 g. (0.1–0.3 oz.) of dried flower heads taken as a decoction. Externally, the decoction is used to wash affected areas.

The leaves of Aztec marigold are used mainly for treating carbuncles, sores, and boils. The usual daily internal dose is 4.5 to 9 g. (0.15–0.3 oz.) of dried leaves taken as a decoction. For external use, the decoction is used to wash the affected areas or the mashed fresh leaves are applied directly.

The whole French marigold plant, also collected and dried in summer or fall, is used in traditional medicine. Said to dissipate heat, it is also used in treating coughs and diarrhea, with a daily internal dose of 9 to 15 g. (0.3–0.5 oz.), taken as a decoction or powder.

Home remedies: Recorded remedies using marigolds are few. The following are two that do not combine marigolds with other herbs.

To treat **toothache** or **sore eyes,** 15 g. (0.5 oz.) of dried flower heads of Aztec marigold are boiled in water and the liquid is drunk.

To treat **whooping cough,** 15 fresh flower heads are boiled in water and the resulting decoction is taken along with red sugar (a type of crude cane sugar).

Availability: Marigolds are widely grown as ornamental herbs in home gardens and are also sold in garden centers or by florists.

MINT

薄荷

General information: Three mints are commercially important—peppermint, spearmint, and cornmint. Peppermint is known botanically as *Mentha piperita,* spearmint as *Mentha spicata,* and cornmint as *Mentha arvensis* or *Mentha haplocalyx,* all belonging to the mint family. They are aromatic perennial herbs with square stems that propagate by runners. Their aboveground parts reach 1 m. (3.3 ft.) high. Spearmint has sessile leaves (no leafstalks) while peppermint and cornmint have petioled and short-petioled leaves respectively. Each mint has numerous varieties and hybrids. Although they all have basically minty smells, these varieties have different proportions of aroma chemicals in their volatile oils, giving them subtly but distinctly different flavors and aromas.

All three mints are cultivated worldwide, but the United States is the major producer of peppermint and spearmint and their oils, while Brazil, China, and Japan are major producers of cornmint and cornmint oil. Dried mint leaves are used as a spice or in teas. The fresh or partially dried whole aboveground herb is used for mint oil production.

The classification of mints is extremely complicated. In addition to their scientific names, each of the mints is also known under other, popular names which need not concern us.

Peppermint and spearmint have been used in the West for thousands of years, for both medicinal and culinary purposes. Medicinally, they are used as pain relievers, muscle relaxants, stimulants, tonics, stomachics, and carminatives for various conditions that include bellyache, indigestion, nausea, diarrhea, sore throat, colds, headaches, toothaches, nervousness, insomnia, cramps, coughs, heartburn, and migraine, among others.

Cornmint, also known as field mint or Japanese mint, is the Chinese counterpart of the two Western mints. It is the mint traditionally used in Chinese medicine, and is known in Chinese as *bo he.*

The mints contain similar chemical constituents, though there are considerable variations in the relative proportions of these compounds among them. They all contain a volatile oil, ranging from about 0.3% or 0.4% in peppermint, to 0.7% in spearmint, and 1% to 2% in cornmint. Among dozens of aroma chemicals present in the volatile oil, menthol, methone, and carvone (which is also found in caraway) are found in the largest amounts. Peppermint oil contains 30% to 50% menthol and 20% to 30% menthone, but only minor amounts of carvone. Spearmint oil, on the other hand, contains 50% to 70% carvone, with only minor amounts of menthol and menthone. The largest concentration of menthol is present in cornmint oil, which normally contains 70% to 95% menthol and 10% to 20% menthone, with only minor quantities of carvone. Due to its high concentrations of menthol, cornmint oil is used for the production of natural menthol. The menthol is in such large amounts that it can be easily separated from the oil by freezing. The resulting "dementholized" oil still contains about 55% menthol and is the dementholized cornmint oil sold commercially. This oil can be used as a further source of menthol.

In addition to volatile oil, mints also contain numerous biologically active constituents, including flavonoids (such as rutin), resins, tannin, and azulene, among others.

In addition to folk medicinal uses, mints and mint oils are extensively used in Western countries as flavorings or fragrance components in all sorts of pharmaceutical and cosmetic preparations, as well as in processed foods. The minty flavor or fragrance in products such as cough lozenges and syrups, mouthwashes, toothpastes, chewing gums, chocolate mint cookies, and candies is certainly familiar to most people living in the West.

Effects on the body: Mint oils (especially peppermint and cornmint) have germ-killing properties that are due to the menthol they contain. Menthol also has expectorant and antitussive as well as anticonvulsant effects on experimental animals and in humans. When applied locally, menthol has been reported to stop headache, neuralgia, and itching.

Despite these properties, menthol may cause allergic reactions in some sensitive individuals, such as flushing, contact dermatitis, and headache. Instant collapse of infants has also reportedly occurred when ointment containing menthol was applied to their nostrils to treat cold symptoms. Since peppermint and cornmint both contain sizable amounts of menthol, one should be cautious when using these mints or their oils.

Azulene isolated from peppermint has been found to reduce inflammation in laboratory animals. This compound, or its derivatives (e.g., chamazulene), is also present in such well-known herbs as chamomile, and is used to treat inflammations, among other conditions.

Traditional uses: Although cornmint is the mint normally used in traditional medicine, spearmint is also used occasionally. However, the use of peppermint in traditional Chinese medicine has not been recorded. The dried aboveground parts of cornmint constitute the drug.

The medicinal use of cornmint was first described in the *Tang Ben Cao,* a well-known herbal of the Tang Dynasty written in the middle of the 7th century. According to its authors, cornmint could be found everywhere, indicating that it was no newcomer even at that time. On the other hand, the medicinal use of spearmint in China is of only recent origin.

Cornmint is traditionally considered to have cooling qualities, while spearmint is considered to be warming. They are therefore used for somewhat different purposes.

Cornmint is an officially recognized drug in the People's Republic of China, being currently listed in its pharmacopeia. It is used for colds, headaches, bloodshot eyes, sore throat, sores of the mouth and tongue, toothache, hives, measles, and rash, among other ailments. It is usually taken as a tea, which is prepared by boiling the mint in water for a short period of time (three to five minutes). Prolonged boiling is said to destroy its potency. The usual daily oral dose is 2.5 to 6 g. (0.1–0.2 oz.) of the dried herb and 15 to 31 g. (0.5–1.1 oz.) of the fresh.

Spearmint is used mainly for treating colds, cough, headache, painful menstruation, and abdominal distention and pain. The dosage is the same as that of cornmint.

For external uses, the fresh mints are mashed and applied directly, or the dried mints are boiled in water and the resulting decoction is used for washing affected areas.

Home remedies: All the recorded remedies are based on cornmint. However, if cornmint is not readily available, peppermint is the closest substitute, as it contains chemical constituents more akin to those of cornmint than does spearmint.

To treat **bloody dysentery,** a recipe from an early 15th-century herbal calls for simply drinking a decoction of cornmint.

According to an 8th-century remedy for **bee stings** and **insect bites,** fresh cornmint is mashed and applied directly to the affected areas.

To treat **earache,** a folk remedy from southern China directs one to express the juice from fresh cornmint leaves and stems and drop this juice into the aching ear. When used as a nose drop, this juice can also be used to stop **nosebleeds,** according to a traditional recipe.

To treat **rhinitis** (inflammation of the mucous membranes of the nose), **nasal sinusitis,** or **nasal congestion** due to colds, a modern practical herbal gives the following recipe: 9 g. (0.3 oz.) dried cornmint, 3 g. (0.1 oz.) borax, and 1 g. (0.04 oz.) borneol (a crystalline alcohol) are mixed well and ground to a fine powder. A small amount of this powder is snuffed three times daily.

Availability: Dried cornmint is available from Chinese herb shops as *bo he.* Dried peppermint and spearmint leaves are sold in health food stores and in supermarkets as tea. Fresh mint can be easily grown in home gardens.

MUNG BEAN

绿豆

General information: Although mung beans are among the most common food products in the Chinese diet and are consumed in various forms, bean sprouts and bean threads are probably the two forms with which Westerners are most familiar. The former are germinated mung beans (see Soybean), while the latter are noodles made from mung-bean flour.

Because of their green color, mung beans are known in Chinese as *lu dou,* meaning "green beans." Botanically, the mung bean plant is known as *Phaseolus radiatus, Phaseolus aureus, Vigna radiata,* or *Phaseolus mungo* of the pea family. It is an annual herb, erect or slightly twining at the tips, grows to about 1 m. (3 ft.) tall, and is cultivated throughout China, India, Japan, the Philippines, and other Asian countries. The seeds (mung beans) are only 4 to 6 mm. (about 0.2 in.) long and are the source of several food and medicinal products including bean flour, bean skin, bean sprouts, and bean threads. Other parts of the mung bean plant, including the leaves and flowers, are also used in Chinese medicine.

Bean sprouts are prepared by soaking mung beans in fresh water until they germinate and the sprouts reach about 5 cm. (2 in.) long.

Mung beans contain large amounts of carbohydrates (60%), proteins (24%), and potassium (1%) and small amounts of fat (1%) and sodium (0.006%). They also contain other minerals, vitamins, and biologically active constituents commonly present in beans.

Cooked bean sprouts (drained) contain about 91% water, 3%

proteins, 5% carbohydrates, 0.2% fats, minerals, and vitamins, as well as other biologically active constituents. Due to their unpleasant flavor when uncooked, bean sprouts, like soybean sprouts, are rarely eaten raw by the Chinese.

Effects on the body: In recent years, scientific research in India and China has shown that mung beans can lower lipid levels in the blood of laboratory animals. A report from the Nanjing Medical College, published in a 1981 issue of the *Chinese Journal of Cardiovascular Diseases,* describes the successful prevention and treatment of induced hyperlipemia (excessive fat in the blood) and atherosclerosis in rabbits, using mung beans and young bean sprouts. These findings indicate that mung beans and bean sprouts may be useful in the prevention and treatment of heart diseases in humans.

Traditional uses: Although mung beans are commonly used as food in Chinese communities, they are also often eaten with therapeutic intentions. In Chinese medicine, the two most important properties of mung beans and of their derivatives are their abilities to dissipate heat and to detoxify the body. Thus, traditionally, mung beans are used in summer for cooling down as well as in treating such toxic conditions as swelling, boils, sores, carbuncles, erysipelas, and dysentery. Some of these uses date back to the middle of the 7th century, during the Tang Dynasty. In addition, mung beans have also been traditionally used in treating drug poisoning and poisoning due to lead, coal, and alcohol. For these purposes the beans are sometimes used with licorice. Thus, for treating aconite poisoning, a decoction of 112 g. (4 oz.) of mung beans and 56 g. (2 oz.) of licorice is drunk.

The medicinal properties of bean sprouts, like those of mung beans, are detoxifying and heat-dissipating; their medicinal uses are also similar. When used as a food, bean sprouts are usually cooked briefly. For medicinal purposes, however, they are decocted. The daily internal dose is 84 to 112 g. (3–4 oz.).

Mung-bean skins—the seed coats of mung beans—are generally produced as a by-product of bean-sprout production. After the beans have sprouted, the skins fall off and are collected and sun-dried. The dried drug is light brown and has very little taste. The medicinal properties and uses of mung-bean skins are similar to those of mung beans. They are used internally either as a powder or as a decoction, with a daily dose of 5 to 12 g. (0.2–0.4 oz.).

Modern uses: In recent years, the successful clinical use of mung beans has been reported for treating pesticide poisoning, lead poisoning, parotiditis (mumps), and second-degree burns, this last externally, with mung-bean flour, which reportedly promotes healing without scars.

Home remedies: A soup made by boiling mung beans until they are completely broken down and then sweetened with sugar is very popular among Cantonese. When I was growing up in Hong Kong, my family used to eat it quite often in summer. It is not only nutritious but also helps to quench thirst, to cool one down, and to prevent **heat rash** or **prickly heat.**

For treating small but painful **boils** or **sores** on the head and neck area, the following simple home remedy is often used: A small handful of mung beans (1/8–1/4 cup) is boiled with a few cups of water until the skin just starts to come off. The juice is decanted and drunk straight or sweetened with a small amount of sugar. This remedy can be taken once daily for a few days. However, although it appears innocuous, it is not recommended for weak or sick persons, since mung beans themselves, unless well cooked, are considered to have a weakening effect. According to Cantonese folk medicine, if eating deep-fried foods (chicken, potatoes, etc.) does not bother you but eating certain types of vegetables or fruits (watermelon, winter melon, bean sprouts, etc.) makes you feel dizzy or causes diarrhea, then you should not indulge in mung-bean products. On the other hand, if fruits and vegetables do not bother you but deep-fried foods give you dry mouth, dry throat, pimples on the face, or a generally uncomfortable feeling, then mung beans are for you and their weakening effects will not affect you.

Sores and **boils** can also be treated externally with powdered mung beans made into a paste with water. These, when mixed with other Chinese herbs, are also used for facial **blackheads** and **acne.** The mixture is added to warm water to form a paste and applied to the face before bedtime. It is believed to absorb the excess oil that causes such facial problems.

Availability: Mung beans are readily available in Chinese groceries and in many health food stores. Bean sprouts are also sold in some supermarkets.

MUSTARD

芥子

General information: Two kinds of mustard are used in Chinese medicine—white (or yellow) mustard and brown mustard. White mustard is known scientifically as *Brassica alba, Brassica hirta,* or *Sinapis alba,* and brown mustard as *Brassica juncea* or *Sinapis juncea.* Brown mustard seeds are known in Chinese as *jie zi* and white mustard seeds as *bai jie zi.* Both are annual or biennial herbs, up to about 1 m. (3.3 ft.) high, belonging to the mustard family. White mustard is believed to be a native of the Mediterranean region, while brown mustard is a native of Asia. They are now cultivated worldwide. Although another mustard, black mustard *(Brassica nigra),* is also used as a common spice, it is not used in Chinese medicine.

The pungent taste and tear-producing properties of mustard seeds are due to nitrogen- and sulfur-containing compounds called isothiocyanates. These compounds are formed from glucosides called sinigrin (present in brown mustard) and sinalbin (in white mustard), which are normally present in ground mustard seeds when the seeds are dry. Once water is added, however, special enzymes (e.g., myrosin), also present in the seeds, break down these glucosides to form isothiocyanates. That is why dry mustard powder has no pungent odor, which it develops only shortly after water or vinegar is added. Commercial ground mustard (mustard flour) often contains a mixture of brown and white mustard seeds. The more pungent (hot) types of mustard flour are produced by first removing the fixed oil (fat) present in the mustard seeds. This oil accounts for over one-third the weight of the seeds but does not contribute to their aroma or taste.

Except for sinigrin and sinalbin, present in brown mustard and white mustard respectively, the two types of mustard seeds have similar chemical constituents. Both contain sizable amounts (25%–37%) of fats, proteins, mucilage, and numerous other biologically active compounds. Brown mustard yields a volatile oil (about 1%) composed almost exclusively of allyl isothiocyanate, which is formed from the breakdown of sinigrin. On the other hand, white mustard does not yield a volatile oil because in it sinalbin is broken down into isothiocyanates that are not volatile.

In Western folk medicine, both brown and white mustard seeds are used in treating rheumatism, arthritis, sciatica, lumbago, and neuralgia. They are also used as emetics, diuretics, stimulants, appetizers, and rubefacients.

Mustard oil is an active ingredient in some commercial dog and cat repellents.

Effects on the body: Mustard oil (allyl isothiocyanate) is very irritating to the skin, producing blisters. It is also tear-producing and is considered to be one of the most toxic volatile oils. Hence, one should be cautious when handling mustard flour, which produces this oil when it is wet.

Traditional uses: Mustard has been used in Chinese medicine for many centuries, first having been described in a well-known herbal of the early 6th century. However, the records are not clear about whether both brown and white mustards have a long history of use, or only brown mustard.

For both mustards, the seeds are harvested in late summer or early autumn, when the pods are just ripe but have not opened. The whole plant is pulled out and after drying under the sun it is thrashed to set free the seeds which are then separated from dirt and other plant parts by sifting and picking.

Traditionally, both mustards are considered to have similar properties, being pungent-tasting, warming, and nontoxic to slightly toxic. They are used to treat vomiting, coughing, stomachache, bellyache, numb feet, rheumatism, and traumatic injuries, among other conditions. The usual daily internal dose is 3 to 9 g. (0.1–0.3 oz.) used as a decoction or in the form of a powder or pills. Externally, the powder is applied directly to affected areas as a poultice.

Modern uses: During the past decade, the Chinese have tried using mustard for chronic bronchitis and knee pain.

For chronic bronchitis, they have used a 10% or 20% solution made from white mustard seeds and injected it into various selected acupuncture points. They have found this treatment effective for 76% to 85% of the approximately 300 patients treated.

For knee pain with swelling, 62 g. (2.2 oz.) of white mustard powder was mixed with an amount of liquor adequate to form a paste which was then applied to the knee. A new application was made when the old one dried. Treatment was continued until blisters started to appear. This method was tried with two patients, both of whom responded to the treatment.

Home remedies: Many remedies based on mustard seeds (especially brown mustard) are found in classical herbals, but most are somewhat complicated. Two simpler ones are given here.

To treat **carbuncles** and **swelling,** a 7th-century recipe calls for mixing brown mustard-seed powder with a little water, placing the resultant paste on a piece of paper and applying it to the affected part.

For the treatment of **scrofula** (swelling of the lymph nodes of the neck), brown mustard-seed powder is mixed with a small amount of vinegar and formed into patties which are placed directly over the scrofula. In order not to injure underlying flesh, the mustard patty should be removed as soon as inflammation subsides. This recipe is also from a classical herbal.

Availability: Mustard flour (powder) is available as a spice in grocery stores and supermarkets. Mustard seeds are available from some specialty stores and from Chinese herb shops.

NUTMEG

肉豆蔻

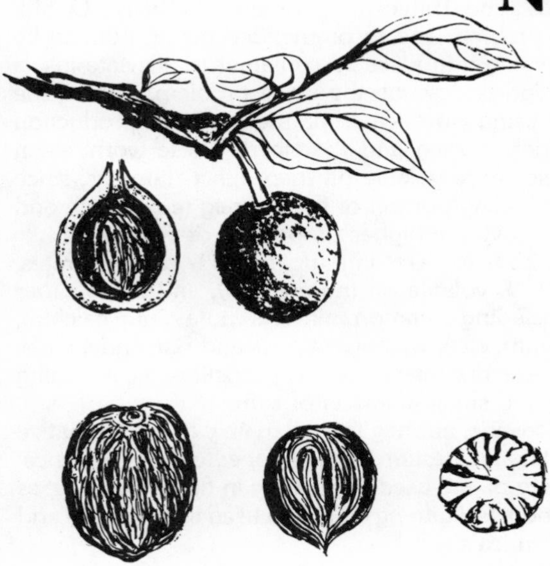

General information: Known in both the West and the East for centuries, nutmeg today is widely used as a spice in the Western world. What immediately comes to mind is its common use in egg-nog, especially around Christmas time. For this purpose, a pinch of it is simply sprinkled into a glass of eggnog. Nutmeg is also used by some fun-seekers for getting high, and produces hallucinations and euphoria, but this practice is extremely dangerous since large doses of nutmeg can be fatal.

Nutmeg is the seed of the nutmeg tree, known scientifically as *Myristica fragrans* of the nutmeg family. It is called *rou dou kou* in Chinese. An evergreen, with spreading branches and dense foliage, the tree reaches a height of about 20 m. (66 ft.). A native of the Molucca Islands of Indonesia, nutmeg is now cultivated in many tropical regions, but is produced commercially mainly in Indonesia and the island of Grenada in the West Indies. Small amounts are also produced in southern Chinese provinces, including Sichuan, Guang-dong, and Guangxi. Its fleshy fruit grows to a length of about 6 cm. (2.4 in.), which on ripening splits in half, exposing a bright red netlike appendage (called aril) wrapped around a dark reddish-brown shell. Inside the shell is a single seed which, after drying, constitutes nut-meg. The dried netlike aril is mace, another well-known spice.

Nutmeg is prone to insect attack, and this situation has not changed for centuries. The 16th-century Chinese herbalist, Li Shizhen, described this problem and recommended drying nutmeg by heat, followed by keeping it in a sealed container to alleviate insect problems. Modern reports describe the same problem. In fact, the common practice of using worm-eaten nutmegs for the production of nutmeg oil is widely known and described. These worm-eaten nutmegs actually yield more volatile oil than intact nutmegs, since much of the non-oil-yielding portion of the nutmeg (e.g., starch and fats) has been eaten, leaving a higher proportion of volatile oil.

Nutmeg contains 25% to 40% fats, up to 50% carbohydrates, about 6% proteins, 10% volatile oil (nutmeg oil), and many other minor constituents including common minerals (potassium, calcium, phosphorus, magnesium, etc.), vitamins (e.g., A and Bs), and sterols. Nutmeg oil also contains dozens of chemical constituents, including 4% to 8% myristicin and small amounts of safrole.

In Western folk medicine, nutmeg is used mainly as a carminative and stimulant in treating indigestion, lack of appetite, and flatulence.

Nutmeg and nutmeg oil are used extensively in flavoring all types of processed food products. Nutmeg oil is also used in cosmetics and in flavoring pharmaceuticals.

Effects on the body: Ingestion of large doses of nutmeg (e.g., 7 to 8 g., or ¼ oz.) can produce hallucinations, euphoria, feelings of unreality, stupor, disorientation, and fast heartbeat, as well as stomachache, nausea, and vomiting. Deaths resulting from the ingestion of large doses of nutmeg have been reported. The hallucinogenic and other psychotropic qualities of nutmeg are believed to be due to myristicin.

Traditional uses: The use of nutmeg in Chinese medicine dates back to around the 5th century A.D. It has since been described in most major Chinese herbals.

In addition to the simple, dried, raw nutmeg (the spice), numerous types of cooked or heat-treated nutmegs are used in Chinese medicine. There are at least a dozen ways of preparing nutmeg for medicinal uses. The resulting products have different chemical compositions and different therapeutic potencies. An article that appeared in the *Journal of Chinese Materia Medica* in 1982 describes the history and methods of preparing nutmeg, its chemical composition, how it is affected by these methods of preparation, its resulting therapeutic qualities, and problems relating to modern scientific studies on nutmeg preparations. In their conclusion, the authors warn against an easy, simple-minded approach to studying Chinese drugs, such as using criteria based only on chemical or pharmacological findings.

They stress the need to base conclusions on findings from a combination of different scientific disciplines.

Nutmeg is considered to be beneficial to the spleen, stomach, and large intestine. As in Western folk medicine, nutmeg is used in Chinese medicine mostly as an aromatic, carminative, or stomachic. Conditions for which it is most commonly used include vomiting, heartburn, abdominal distention, indigestion, diarrhea, and bellyache. The usual daily oral dose is 1.5 to 4.5 g. (about ⅓–1 teaspoonful) taken as a decoction or powder.

Mace is used for the same purposes as nutmeg and its dosage is also the same.

Nutmeg is seldom used alone in Chinese medicine. Most available recorded remedies call for several herbs in addition to nutmeg.

Availability: Nutmeg is sold as a spice in groceries, supermarkets, and spice shops. It is also available from Chinese herb shops.

PAPAYA

番木瓜

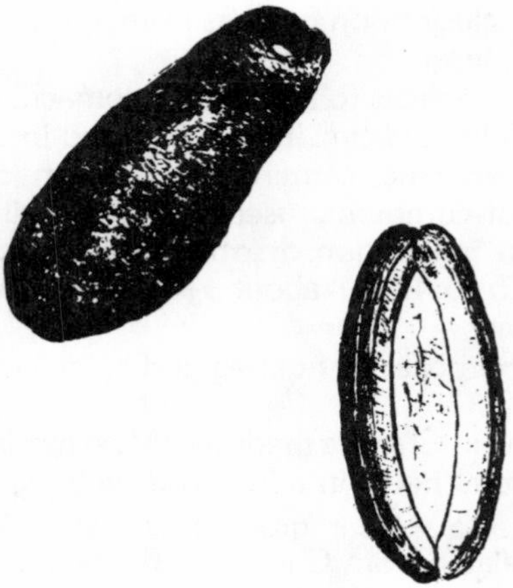

General information: Also known as pawpaw or papaw, papaya is a native of tropical America. Botanically it is called *Carica papaya* of the papaya or pawpaw family. It is known as *fan mu gua* in Chinese, with *fan,* meaning "foreign," denoting its probable introduction to China by way of the Philippines. Although a tree that reaches 10 m. (33 ft.) in height, papaya can best be described as a giant herb, the reason being that it does not have a trunk with solid wood like that of most trees. Instead, its trunk is soft, like that of a herbaceous plant. The papaya tree trunk is erect and seldom branched, with many leaf scars and usually a terminal crown of large palmate leaves with seven to nine deep lobes. The leaves reach 60 cm. (2 ft.) across and are borne on hollow petioles that are 60 cm. (2 ft.) or more long. The papaya plant flowers year-round in the tropics, producing melonlike fruits that range in shape from oblong to almost spherical, depending on the cultivated forms. The fruits are yellow or orange-yellow when ripe and measure 10 to 30 cm. (4–12 in.) long. The ripe fruits are sweet and have a unique flavor; they are a popular food in the tropics. The unripe fruits are not sweet and taste somewhat bland but are also eaten, boiled or cooked as a vegetable or pickled.

Papaya is now grown in many tropical and subtropical regions, especially Central America, the West Indies, Africa (e.g., Uganda and Tanzania), Hawaii, India, Sri Lanka, Malaysia, Indonesia, and China. It grows best on rich, loamy, but well-drained soil. Although grown mainly for its fruit, to be used for direct consumption, a sizable amount of papaya is cultivated for the production of papain, a meat-digesting enzyme which is widely used in Western countries as a meat tenderizer both commercially and at home. If you read the labels of instant meat tenderizers in the supermarket or on your kitchen shelf you will find papain is the active ingredient. Papain is also used as a digestive aid, in face creams, cleansers, face-lift formulas, dentifrices, as well as in enzyme cleaners for soft contact lenses.

It is common knowledge among peoples of the tropics that cooking meat with a piece of green papaya or wrapped in papaya leaf will make it tender faster. When I was a child my grandmother would sometimes put a piece of green papaya fruit in the pot to cook with the meat. She never learned to read and never heard of papain, but she had learned from her mother to use papaya as a meat tenderizer. This practice was probably introduced to the Orient along with the papaya plant during the 16th and 17th centuries.

Although the meat-tenderizing properties of papaya have been utilized for centuries, it was not until recent years that these qualities were found to be due to papain. This enzyme is present in the white latex, or juice, found throughout the plant, with the largest amounts present in the full-grown but unripe fruit. Commercial papain is prepared from this unripe fruit by scoring it with a sharp razor blade or knife to let the white milky juice ooze out. This juice soon coagulates, forms a soft mass over the cut, and is scraped off and dried under the sun or by artificial heat. The scoring is usually done early in the morning and the whole process is completed by noon. The resulting crude papain is exported from producing countries in the tropics to America or Europe where it is purified for various food, drug, and cosmetic applications.

In addition to papain, fresh papaya contains chymopapain and other enzymes. It also contains trace amounts of an alkaloid (carpaine), a glycoside (carposide), pectin, vitamins A and C (in proportions that are considerably higher than those in bananas or oranges), other vitamins, minerals (calcium, sodium, iron, potassium), 10% carbohydrates, 0.6% protein, and 0.1% fat.

Chymopapain is closely related to papain in its protein-digesting activities, but it is more stable, acid, and heat-resistant than papain. The U.S. Food and Drug Administration (FDA) has recently approved it for direct injection (in solution form) into slipped disks.

Effects on the body: Some scientists have reported papain to have the ability to reduce inflammation and edema, while others have found it to possess no such properties. However, papain is known to have digested dead tissue without affecting the surrounding live tissue, and this ability has gained it a reputation as a "biological scalpel." It can cause allergic reactions, such as hives or shock, in some sensitive individuals, and such people should be cautious when handling or eating papaya.

Carpaine is toxic and has been shown to paralyze the central nervous system, causing the death of mice and rabbits from respiratory paralysis and heart dysfunctions.

Traditional uses: Spaniards are generally credited as the first to have taken papaya seeds to the Philippines (from which the fruit was imported to China), and Captain James Cook is believed to have been the first to introduce the seeds to Hawaii. The date of papaya's introduction to China is not certain, but it was first described in the 16th-century herbal, *Ben Cao Gang Mu,* though the description does not exactly match that of papaya as we know it. Papaya has also been referred to in other traditional herbals as "long-life fruit."

The major traditional uses are in treating indigestion, stomachache, dysentery, constipation, urinary difficulties, rheumatism, and foot ulcers. It is customary to use the green fruit for indigestion and stomachache and to use the ripe fruit for dysentery, constipation, and urinary problems. In either case, the papaya is usually boiled in water and the liquid is drunk. However, the ripe fruit is also eaten directly, raw.

To increase milk flow in nursing mothers, Cantonese cook green papaya fruit with meat and eat it as a vegetable (see below).

Papaya leaves when mashed are applied as a poultice to treat skin ulcers and inflammations.

Home remedies: Although the traditional herbals do not seem to have recorded any specific remedies based on papaya, the Cantonese have many folk medicinal uses for it besides eating it as a fruit or vegetable. The following are two of those remedies as I have remembered them.

To treat **insufficient milk flow** in nursing mothers a small green papaya, about 250 g. (9 oz.), is boiled gently in 2 l. (2 qt.) of water with 57 g. (2 oz.) of lean pork until about a quarter of the liquid remains. This takes about an hour. The resulting milky soup is drunk, and as much of the papaya and pork are eaten as is possible. This soup is usually taken for a few days in a row.

For **constipation,** my family used to recommend two or three slices (probably about ½ lb.) of ripe papaya. Too much papaya may cause diarrhea, however.

Availability: Green and ripe papayas are sold in ethnic grocery stores and some supermarkets, especially in the coastal cities of America.

PEANUT (Groundnut)

花生

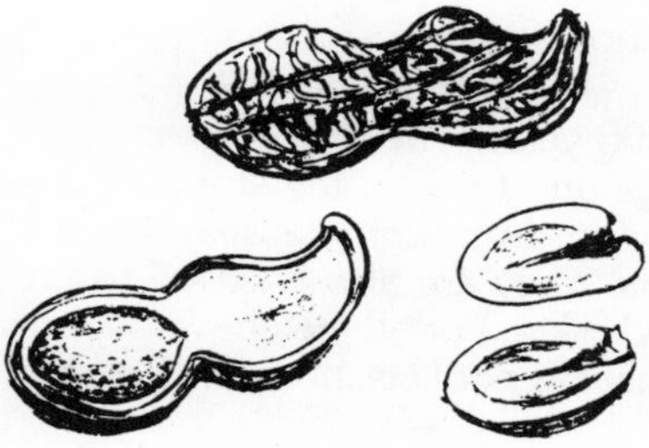

General information: Peanuts, or groundnuts, are among the most widely consumed foods in the world. Native to South America, the peanut plant was introduced into Europe in the 16th century and spread to Asia not long thereafter. Now peanuts are grown in warm regions all over the world. Along with several other countries, the United States, India, and China are major producers of peanuts.

The peanut plant, *Arachis hypogaea,* belongs to the pea family. Its Chinese name is *hua sheng.* Peanut is an annual herb, 25 to 50 cm. (10–20 in.) tall. Although it flowers normally, as other plants do, after the flowers wither the flower stems elongate and enter the ground, where the fruits mature into peanuts. Numerous cultivated varieties produce peanuts of different sizes and shapes as well as subtly different flavors.

Peanuts are very nutritious. When raw, they contain about 26% protein, 48% oil, 19% carbohydrates, minerals, and large amounts of vitamins (e.g., B_1 and niacin). Most of the vitamins are present in the skins. Peanut shells contain active principles that lower blood-pressure and serum-cholesterol levels. Although nutritious, peanuts that are moldy should not be eaten since some of the molds produce toxins that can cause liver cancer.

Roasted peanuts, peanut butter, and peanut oil are just a few of the many peanut products available all over the world. Peanut shells are used in the manufacture of certain chemicals and plastics. They are also used as cattle feed and in fertilizers.

Effects on the body: Scientists have found that peanuts (especially the skin) can stop bleeding in hemophiliacs as well as other types of bleeding conditions, including internal hemorrhages (e.g., of the intestine, stomach, and uterus). However, roasting greatly reduces the effectiveness of peanuts as hemostatics. The active principles that produce these effects are still not known.

Traditional uses: Relative newcomers to Chinese medicine, peanuts have been used for less than 300 years. They have traditionally been considered to soothe the lungs and to calm the stomach and spleen. Their major uses are in treating dry cough, nausea, beriberi, and lack of milk in nursing mothers. They are also believed to improve complexion and to soften one's skin. For all the above medicinal purposes, peanuts are almost always cooked in water. Roasted peanuts are rarely called for.

Modern uses: In modern times the Chinese have found numerous other medicinal uses for peanuts. Peanut skins are now used clinically for treating various types of hemorrhages, chilblains, and chronic bronchitis. These uses have been reported in scientific publications in China and have been found to be quite effective. For example, internal and postoperative bleeding in 80% of 285 patients treated with injections of extract of peanut skin was satisfactorily controlled. The treatment was particularly effective in stomach, intestinal, and uterine bleeding, as well as in bleeding due to hemophilia, surgery, and liver diseases.

In the past few years, reports of the effectiveness of peanut-shell extracts in treating high blood pressure and hyperlipidemia (e.g., high serum cholesterol) have appeared in various regions in China. Chinese scientists have since been trying to identify the active principles responsible for these effects. They have recently identified β-sitosterol and luteolin as serum lipid-lowering and blood-pressure-lowering constituents in peanut shells. Other active constituents remain to be identified.

Home remedies: One of the best-known uses of peanuts is in the treatment of **beriberi,** a disease that affects the lower limbs, causing rigidity and paralysis. Beriberi is a vitamin-deficiency syndrome caused by lack of B_1 (thiamine) and other vitamins in the diet. When I was growing up, it was a status symbol for many Chinese to eat highly polished (the whitest) rice, from which most vitamins had been removed but which was much more expensive than unpolished or poorly polished brands, which contain very high concentrations of B_1 and other vitamins. Consequently, prolonged use of polished rice without obtaining vitamin B_1 from other sources resulted in instances of beriberi, especially among well-to-do Chinese. Although beriberi still occurs in the Far East, it does so rarely in the advanced countries of the West because of extensive vitamin supplementation in rice and other grain products. Nevertheless, if a treatment for beriberi is needed, peanuts (with skins) are boiled in water to form a soup which is drunk. For beriberi at its initial stages, 85 to 115 g. (3–4 oz.) of peanuts are taken four times daily for a few days. For prolonged beriberi, long-term use of 170 to 230 g. (6–8 oz.) daily is called for.

To treat **lack of milk** in nursing mothers, a traditional remedy calls for stewing about 85 g. (3 oz.) of peanuts with one pig's foot and eating the stew.

To treat **excessive phlegm** with or without cough, an 18th-century herbal remedy calls for cooking 57 to 85 g. (2–3 oz.) of peanuts (without skins) briefly in water and eating the soup. Ground or crushed raw peanuts are also said to relieve phlegm. Although raw and boiled peanuts are considered to have phlegm-relieving effects, roasted peanuts are said to have the opposite effect.

Availability: Unroasted raw or dried peanuts are available in Chinese and other ethnic groceries, health food stores, and some supermarkets.

PEPPER (Black and White)

胡椒

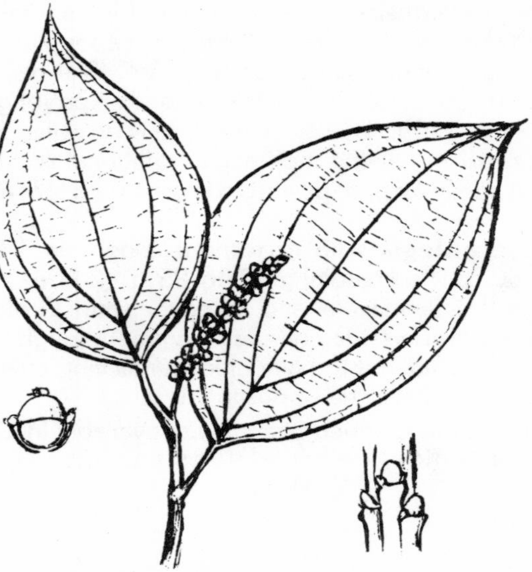

General information: There are two kinds of pepper, black and white. They are not to be confused with hot pepper (see Pepper [Hot]). Both are derived from fruits of the pepper plant, known scientifically as *Piper nigrum* of the pepper family. In Chinese, pepper is known as *hu jiao,* meaning "foreign spice." The pepper plant is a native of southwestern India and is now extensively cultivated in other tropical regions. The plant is a perennial woody vine with many swollen nodes, climbing to about 5 m. (16.5 ft.). It has relatively large oval leaves that measure 8 to 16 cm. (3–6.3 in.) long and 4 to 9 cm. (1.6–3.5 in.) broad. The flowers are borne on spikes that are about 10 cm. (4 in.) long. The fruits are small round berries, red when ripe and 4 to 5 mm. (⅙–⅕ in.) in diameter.

Black pepper is produced from berries that are just beginning to turn red. The whole spikes of berries are cut and dried under the sun or by artificial heat. After the berries are dried, they turn black and wrinkly. They are then removed from the spikes and constitute the black pepper that is sold commercially.

White pepper is produced from berries that have turned completely red. These ripe berries are soaked in water or lime water for several days. The skin (pericarp) is rubbed off and after being washed, the skinless berries are dried under the sun to yield the grayish-white product called white pepper.

China, Malaysia, India, and Indonesia are some of the major producers of pepper.

Both black and white peppers are widely used as spices throughout the world. Black pepper is more aromatic, but white pepper has a more delicate flavor. The Chinese prefer white pepper, while Westerners seem to prefer black pepper.

Black pepper contains 2% to 4% volatile oil, while white pepper contains only a trace amount, since most of the volatile oil is present in the skin of the berry, which is removed in white pepper. This volatile oil is composed of dozens of aromatic chemicals, including monoterpenes and sesquiterpenes. However, it does not contain the pungent principles of pepper, which are alkaloids.

Except for the difference in their volatile-oil content, both black and white peppers contain essentially the same chemical constituents. They include 5% to 9% alkaloids, two of which (piperine and piperanine) are the known pungent principles. According to analyses by the U.S. Department of Agriculture, black pepper also contains 10.95% protein, 64.81% carbohydrates, 3.26% fats, 13.13% fiber, small amounts of minerals, including 12,590 ppm (parts per million), or 1.26%, potassium, 4,370 ppm calcium, 1,940 ppm magnesium, 1,730 ppm phosphorus, 440 ppm sodium, 289 ppm iron, 14 ppm zinc, and small amounts of vitamins (e.g., A, niacin, riboflavin, and thiamine). In comparison, white pepper contains 10.40% protein, 68.61% carbohydrates, 2.12% fats, 4.34% fiber, minerals (730 ppm potassium, 2,650 ppm calcium, 900 ppm magnesium, 1,760 ppm phosphorus, 50 ppm sodium, 143 ppm iron, and 11 ppm zinc), and trace amounts of vitamins.

Although a popular spice present in many processed foods and available on practically every meal table in Western countries, pepper is rarely used as a folk medicine in the West. It is used only occasionally, as a stimulant, carminative, or tonic.

Effects on the body: Pepper has diaphoretic, carminative, and diuretic properties. It also increases gastric secretion and promotes stomach and intestinal peristalsis.

In an experiment conducted in China in the late 1950s, 24 healthy subjects were asked to chew 0.1 g. (a few berries) of pepper without swallowing it. Their blood pressure was monitored before, during, and after chewing the pepper. It was found that the blood pressure of all 24 subjects was increased while they were chewing the pepper, with an average increase of 13.1 mm. mercury in systolic pressure and 18.1 mm. mercury in diastolic pressure. Their pulse rate was not significantly affected. Ten to 15 minutes after chewing the pepper, blood pressure in all subjects returned to normal. It is not known whether this temporary increase in blood pressure was due to purely physiological factors, stress resulting from the burning sensation on the tongue, or heat felt by the head and body.

Pepper is also irritant to the nose, eyes, and skin.

Traditional uses: Pepper was introduced into China from the West, and its medicinal uses were first described in one of the famous herbals of the Tang Dynasty in the middle of the 7th century.

Traditionally, pepper is considered to have the ability to remove phlegm and gas and to invigorate and detoxify the body. It acts on the stomach and large intestine. Its major uses are in treating conditions of the gastrointestinal tract, including stomachache, nausea, vomiting, diarrhea, dysentery, indigestion, and lack of appetite. However, its uses for other conditions, such as malaria, cholera, asthma in children, toothache, epilepsy, cramps due to calcium deficiency, aching body and limbs, chilblains, and centipede bites have also been recorded. Although black pepper is officially listed in the pharmacopeia of the People's Republic of China, white pepper is more commonly used. When taken internally, the usual daily dose is 1.5 to 3 g. (0.05–0.1 oz.), as a decoction or in the form of pills or powders.

Modern uses: In recent years, numerous reports on the successful clinical use of pepper in treating various conditions have appeared in Chinese health and medical journals. These uses included the treatment of nephritis (inflammation of kidney), neurasthenia, diarrhea in children due to indigestion, chronic tracheitis, wheezing, and various types of skin diseases. Most of these uses involved local application of pepper (as a poutice or cut in half and with the open end against the skin) to selected acupuncture points.

In treating diarrhea in children due to indigestion, a treatment that did not involve acupuncture points included mixing 1 g. (0.04 oz.) freshly ground white pepper with 9 g. (0.3 oz.) glucose powder. For children under one year of age, 0.3 to 0.5 g. of the mixture was given three times daily; for children between one and three years old, 0.5 to 1.5 g. The treatment lasted one to three days. Among 20 patients treated in this manner, 18 were cured and two showed improvement.

In an experiment on treating nephritis with white pepper, seven pepper berries and one chicken egg were used. A small hole was first made in the eggshell. The pepper berries were introduced into the egg through the hole, which was then sealed with flour. After wrapping the egg in wet paper, it was placed on a steaming rack and cooked by steaming. The cooked egg (after being peeled) and the pepper berries were eaten. Adult patients ate two eggs, while children ate one egg, daily. Each treatment course lasted ten days, with three days of rest in between. Of six patients treated by this method, five were cured after three courses of treatment. The sixth patient had chronic nephritis of ten years' duration and did not respond as the others had.

Home remedies: Both classical and recent herbals record numerous remedies based on pepper.

In a recent recipe from Inner Mongolia, white pepper along with chicken eggshell is used to treat **cramps** due to **calcium deficiency.** Twenty pepper berries and two eggshells are baked in an oven until they turn light brown. They are then ground to a powder, mixed well, and divided into 14 equal portions. One portion is taken with boiled water each day until all 14 portions have been taken.

Another recent recipe from Inner Mongolia is for the treatment of **chilblains** or **frostbite.** It can be prepared by soaking 30 g. (1.1 oz.) of whole pepper berries in 300 ml. (10 fl. oz.) of white wine for seven days, then filtering or straining. The resulting infusion is painted on the affected areas once daily.

To treat **nausea** and **vomiting,** a 10th-century remedy calls for boiling 1 g. (0.04 oz.) pepper powder and 31 g. (1.1 oz.) coarsely chopped fresh ginger root in two large cupfuls of water until the mixture is boiled down to half the volume. After straining off the solids, the liquid is taken in three equal doses throughout the day.

In the October 1982 issue of the *Journal of New Chinese Medicine,* the following two recipes (based on traditional herbals) for treating **stomachache** are given. Both make use of pepper.

The first recipe calls for five pepper berries (preferably white) and one chicken egg. The berries are ground to a powder which is mixed well with the egg. The egg is then scrambled in vegetable oil. A small amount of salt is added to taste, and the mixture is eaten as part of the daily meal for a few days.

The second recipe calls for one pig's stomach and 5 g. (0.18 oz.) white pepper. After the pig's stomach is thoroughly cleaned, the pepper berries are placed inside and the stomach is stewed in water in a covered pot until tender. The pepper berries are then removed and salt is added to taste. The soup is drunk, but only part of the meat is eaten, since too much pig stomach may cause digestive problems in some individuals.

The foregoing recipes are not to be used for individuals who have bleeding ulcers of the stomach or intestines, hemorrhoids, or for pregnant women.

Availability: Both black and white peppers are readily available in grocery stores and supermarkets.

PEPPER (Hot)

辣椒

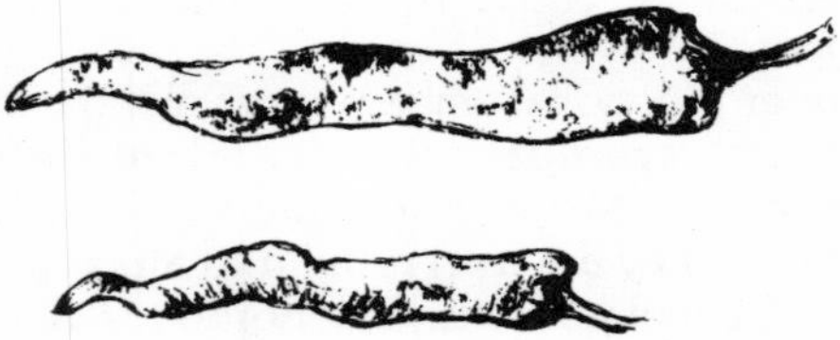

General information: Hot pepper is known under several names —capsicum, cayenne pepper, chili pepper, and tabasco pepper. Its numerous varieties have one thing in common—their hot, pungent taste. Depending on the variety, the taste varies from mildly pungent to extremely pungent.

Imported within the last few hundred years to China, hot pepper was originally called *fan jiao,* or "barbarian's spice." (Just as whites used to call all nonwhites savages, the Chinese called all people outside China barbarians.) Hot pepper was later called *la qie,* "pungent eggplant," because of its resemblance to the shape of an eggplant, and is now more commonly known as *la jiao* ("pungent spice").

Botanically, hot pepper is the fruit of *Capsicum annuum, Capsicum frutescens,* or other *Capsicum* species of the nightshade family. *Capsicum annuum* is an annual herb up to 1 m. (3 ft.) tall, but the other species are usually perennial shrubs. They are all native to tropical America and are now grown all over the world. Some varieties of *C. annuum* produce hot pepper, while other varieties of the same plant yield nonpungent fruits which are known as green pepper, paprika, bell pepper, or sweet pepper.

Hot peppers are widely used in seasoning foods and in folk medicine. The most common forms in which they are used for home seasoning are ground, pickled, and as tabasco sauce. Ground pepper soaked in vegetable oil is also a favorite of many Chinese. In America, extracts of hot pepper known as capsicum extracts, or oleoresin, are widely used in processed foods, including meat products, desserts, baked goods, alcoholic and nonalcoholic beverages. They also used to be popular components of some topical pharmaceutical preparations for treating arthritis, rheumatism, neuralgia, and lumbago but are now seldom used for these purposes in America. However, one can still find them used in certain commercial preparations for stopping thumb sucking or nail biting in children.

The pungent taste of hot pepper is due to its constituent capsaicin and its derivatives. Their concentrations in dried hot pepper range from less than 0.1% (mildly hot) to 1.5% (extremely hot). Dried hot pepper also contains about 13% protein, 9% fat, 60% carbohydrates, minerals, and an exceptionally large amount of vitamin A (close to the amount present in dehydrated carrots). Fresh hot pepper also contains a large amount of vitamin C (several times that in oranges) most of which is destroyed during the drying process. In order to benefit from the high nutritive value of hot pepper one has to have numbed tastebuds, since ordinarily one can hardly ingest enough hot pepper for it to be a worthwhile source of nutrients.

In traditional Western folk medicine, hot pepper is used internally to stimulate appetite and aid digestion, and generally as a tonic. Externally, it is used as a counterirritant in the treatment of rheumatism, arthritis, and other inflammatory conditions.

Effects on the body: Hot pepper is a strong local stimulant or irritant to the skin, mucous membranes, and eyes. The smoke of burning hot pepper is especially irritating to the mucous membranes and was once used for torture in the Malay Peninsula. Prolonged contact with hot pepper or its extracts can result in dermatitis. Hot pepper also caused tumors in the livers of experimental rats when the rats were fed a diet that contained 10% hot pepper. All these undesirable effects of hot pepper are mentioned here to remind you to use it with moderation.

Traditional uses: In Chinese medicine, hot pepper is generally used in the dried form; the ripe fruit is collected in late summer or early autumn and is usually sun-dried. It is traditionally used to increase appetite, to aid digestion, and to treat arthritis and rheumatism, as in Western folk medicine. In addition, it is used in treating abdominal pain, vomiting, diarrhea, chilblains, ringworm, malaria, poisonous snakebite, bruises, and hematomas.

Modern uses: The use of hot pepper for treating chilblains has been well documented, first in an 18th-century herbal, then in later herbals, and finally in modern Chinese medical journals. In modern usage, for treating chilblains and frostbite, a weak decoction or water extract of the pepper is used before the blisters break. This can be prepared by boiling 30 g. (1 oz.) of hot pepper (cut up) in 2,000 to 3,000 ml. (2–3 qt.) of water for three to five minutes and straining off the residue. The liquid is used while still warm to wash the affected areas. Alternatively, an ointment prepared from 30 g. (about 1 oz.) ground hot pepper with seeds, 15 g. (about 0.5 oz.) camphor, and 250 g. (8.8 oz.)

Vaseline can be used. The ointment is rubbed on the chilblains or frostbite until a local burning sensation is felt. In one report, in a medical journal from northeastern China, of 200 patients treated with a weak hot-pepper decoction once daily for up to eleven days (but mostly for under five days), 188 were reported cured, eight had some response, while four did not respond. Best results were obtained with chilblains or frostbite of the hands and feet.

To treat traumatic injuries such as bruises and sprains causing hematomas (swellings containing blood) or swollen and painful joints, an ointment made with one part ground hot pepper and five parts Vaseline is used. Prepared by adding the ground hot pepper to the melted Vaseline, which is then mixed well and cooled until it congeals, this ointment is applied once daily, or once every two days, directly to the injured area. In a 1965 report from a journal of traditional medicine from Zhejiang, seven of 12 patients thus treated were cured and three improved, while two did not respond to this treatment. In the effective cases, four to nine applications were usually used.

In addition to uses above, modern Chinese medicine also uses hot pepper externally to treat parotiditis (mumps) and leg ulcers.

The usual internal daily dose of hot pepper is 1 to 2.5 g (0.04–0.09 oz.). It should not be taken by persons with any of the following conditions: sores, boils, toothache, eye diseases, or hemorrhoids.

Home remedies: One of the old remedies for treating **chilblains** calls for simply peeling off the skin of hot pepper and leaving it directly on the chilblain.

The use of hot pepper in the treatment of poisonous **snakebite** is described in a 19th-century herbal. For this purpose, it recommended that the bitten person simply chew 11 to 12 whole hot peppers and the pain and swelling would subside. Blisters would appear and a yellow liquid would exude from the wounded area while the patient was healing. Alternatively, the hot pepper could be chewed into a mash and then applied directly to the wound with the same effects. Instead of the usual pungent taste, the patient would find the hot pepper to taste sweet. I wonder how much truth there is in this century-old record. If it were true, the hot pepper must react with the snake venom to change the physiology of the tastebuds.

Availability: Hot pepper is readily available in groceries and supermarkets.

ROSE

玫瑰花

General information: There are many kinds of roses, several of which are used in Chinese medicine. Among them are the flowers of the rugosa or rugose (wrinkled) rose and the multiflora (many-flowered) rose. The rugosa rose is known botanically as *Rosa rugosa* and the multiflora rose as *Rosa multiflora,* both belonging to the rose family. Rugosa rose flower is known in Chinese as *mei gui hua,* and multiflora rose flower as *qiang wei hua.* Native to eastern Asia, both roses have been introduced into America and are now found throughout much of eastern Canada and the United States.

The rugosa rose is a sturdy, hardy, leafy shrub growing up to 2 m. (6.6 ft.) high. Its stiff stems are densely covered with bristles and prickles of different sizes, and its leaves have five to nine leaflets that are thick and rugose, measuring 2.5 to 5 cm. (1–2 in.) long. The stipules (appendages borne at base of leaf) are broad and leafy. The flowers are purple or white, very fragrant, and come one to a few in a cluster, measuring 7 to 12 cm. (2.8–4.7 in.) across when fully opened. The brick-red rose hips are large, up to 2.5 cm. (1 in.) or more in diameter, crowned with the long (2.5–4.5 cm., or 1–1.8 in.) spreading sepals. This plant flowers from May through August and fruits between June and September. For the purposes of Chinese medicine the flower buds are collected when they just start to open. They are usually dried by artificial heat, which preserves most of their color and fragrance. Sun-dried flowers are inferior in color and fragrance.

The multiflora rose is a trailing or climbing prickly bush. Its leaves have five to 11 (usually seven or nine) leaflets that measure 2 to 4 cm. (0.8–1.6 in.) long. The stipules are prominent, fringed, or comblike. Its fragrant white flowers are borne 25 to more than 100 to a cluster (hence the name multiflora); they measure 2 to 4 cm. (0.8–1.6 in.) across when fully opened. The brown-red hips are small, usually less than 6 mm. (0.25 in.) in diameter. This rose flowers from May through July and fruits in August and September. For medicinal use, the flowers are collected when they are fully opened, usually on a sunny day, and are dried under the sun.

Rose flowers in general contain traces of volatile oil that accounts for their fragrance. This rose oil contains many aroma chemicals, with citronellol as its major constituent. Other important chemicals include geraniol, nerol, and eugenol. Rose flowers also contain flavonoids (e.g., quercitrin), tannins, β-carotene, and other pigments.

Effects on the body: A decoction of rose flowers was found by Chinese scientists to eliminate the toxic effects of antimony preparations when given to laboratory mice.

When added to food, rose oil has been found to increase the excretion of bile by the liver in cats.

Traditional uses: Although rugosa-rose flower is native to China, its first recorded use in traditional medicine dates back only a few hundred years. Traditionally, it is considered both sweet and slightly bitter and to have warming properties. It is said to have the ability to regulate energy flow, normalize menstrual disturbances, and resolve stasis in the body. One of the official drugs listed in the pharmacopeia of the People's Republic of China, rugosa-rose flower is used mainly for treating stomach conditions (e.g., stomachache due to swelling, gastric neurosis, and chronic gastritis) and menstrual disorders (e.g., irregular and painful periods). It is also used to treat pink and white vaginal discharge, dysentery, rheumatic or rheumatoid arthritis marked by migratory pains, mastitis, sprains, and swellings. The usual internal daily dose is 1.5 to 6 g. (0.05–0.2 oz.) taken as a decoction or powder.

Multiflora-rose flower has a much longer history of use than rugosa-rose flower, although today it is not as often used and is not currently listed in the pharmacopeia of the People's Republic of China. It is considered sweet-tasting and to have cooling properties. It is said to dissipate summer heat, calm the stomach, and stop bleeding. Conditions for which multiflora-rose flower is used include spitting blood due to overheating, dryness in the mouth, excessive thirst, malaria, diarrhea, and external bleeding. The usual internal daily dose is 3 to 6 g. (0.1–0.2 oz.) taken as a decoction. For external use, it is applied directly as a powder.

Home remedies: Rugosa-rose flower is a fairly common folk medicine in China, and is grown around many Chinese homes. There are many recipes using this herb for treating various conditions. A few simple ones are described below.

A well-known 18th-century herbal records a recipe for treating a kind of severe **dysentery** which causes the patient to **lose appetite** and to **vomit** whatever he eats or drinks. The recipe calls for decocting rugosa-rose flowers that have been dried in the shade and then taking the decoction. Since no details on dosage or methods of decoction are given, the normal daily dose and the usual decocting method should apply.

To treat **swellings** or **inflammations,** rugosa-rose flowers (with stems removed), dried by baking under low heat, are ground into a powder and 3 g. (0.1 oz.) of the powder is then taken with wine. This recipe is from a classical herbal.

A folk remedy for treating recurrent **diarrhea** due to chronic **gastritis** calls for the use of fresh or dried rose petals: 3 g. (0.1 oz.) of dried petals (double quantity when fresh petals are used) are steeped for about 10 minutes in a cup of boiling water and the resulting tea is drunk. This tea is prepared and taken twice a day for several days.

To treat minor **sprains,** a modern practical herb manual directs one to prepare a rose-flower wine as follows: Soak 15 g. (0.5 oz.) of dried rugosa-rose flowers in 120 ml. (4 fl. oz.) of white wine for four hours and then remove the flowers by straining or filtering. This wine is divided into three portions, and one portion per day is taken for three days.

To treat a condition resulting from summer heat, characterized by **tight chest, thirst, spitting blood, vomiting,** and **lack of appetite,** a modern Shanghai herb manual calls for 5 to 10 g. (0.18–0.35 oz.) of multiflora-rose flowers taken as a decoction.

Availability: Dried flowers are available in Chinese herb shops. When in season, fresh flowers are available from gardens or fields.

ROSEMARY

迷迭香

General information: Rosemary is a common spice and garden herb that is called for in many Western dishes. Scientifically called *Rosmarinus officinalis* of the mint family, and in Chinese *mi die xiang* ("intoxicating fragrance"), the plant is a small evergreen shrub up to 2 m. (6 ft.) tall. The fragrant leaves are thick, leathery, and narrow, measuring about 3.5 cm. (1.5 in.) long and 2 to 4 mm. (about 0.3 in.) wide. When dried, the leaves serve as the spice. Rosemary is a native of the Mediterranean region but is now cultivated throughout the world.

Rosemary spice and rosemary oil are used extensively in processed food products such as baked goods and meat products. Rosemary oil is also used widely in soaps, creams, lotions, and other cosmetics.

Dried rosemary leaves and flowering tops have been used in Western folk medicine since ancient times as a tonic, stimulant, and carminative in treating indigestion, stomach pains, headaches, head colds, and nervous tension. Externally, they are used for rheumatism, scrofulous sores, eczema, bruises, and wounds. An infusion with borax is used as a wash to prevent baldness, dry scaly skin, and dandruff.

Dried rosemary leaves contain about 5% protein, 15% fats, 64% carbohydrates, minerals (e.g., calcium, iron, and magnesium), vitamins (e.g., A and C), about 0.5% volatile oil (rosemary oil), and other biologically active constituents.

Effects on the body: Western scientists have found that extracts of rosemary promote menstrual discharge and hair growth. Rosemary oil kills various types of bacteria, but it is also toxic to humans and can be fatal if taken in large doses. In some individuals, it can cause skin problems, such as contact dermatitis, as well as eye irritations.

Traditional uses: Rosemary was first introduced into China from the West during the early part of the 3d century and its first recorded use in Chinese medicine dates to the middle of the 8th century. It is used traditionally as a stomachic and diaphoretic (promoting perspiration), and in treating headaches. More recent herbals also list its uses in promoting menstrual discharge, calming nerves, and, when used with borax, in preventing early baldness. The usual internal daily dose is 4.7 to 9.4 g. (0.17–0.34 oz.) boiled with water. When burned with *qiang huo* (*Notopterygium* root), rosemary is traditionally used to repel mosquitoes and gnats.

Availability: Rosemary is widely available as a spice in groceries and supermarkets. It is also available as a garden herb from home gardens.

SAFFRON

番红花

General information: A popular ingredient in some well-known Spanish and French dishes (e.g., paella, arroz con pollo, and bouillabaisse), saffron is probably the most expensive spice. It is derived from saffron crocus, a perennial herb called scientifically *Crocus sativus* of the iris family.

In Chinese, saffron is generally known under two names, *zang hong hua* and *fan hong hua.* The former means "Tibetan red flower" while the latter means "foreign red flower" or "barbarian's red flower." The plant, a native of the eastern Mediterranean region, has a large fleshy corm (bulblike structure) from which leaves and flowers are produced in autumn. It is now cultivated worldwide as an annual or perennial. The plant is sometimes erroneously referred to as autumn crocus; the latter is known scientifically as *Colchicum autumnale* of the lily family and is also called meadow saffron. Meadow saffron is a poisonous plant formerly used in treating gout, rheumatism, and other conditions. The spice saffron consists of the dried stigmas of the saffron crocus. To obtain this spice, the stigmas are hand picked from each flower. An estimated 100,000 to 140,000 flowers are required to yield 1 kg. (2.2 lb.) of saffron, which is produced mainly in Spain, France, Turkey, and India.

Saffron contains about 2% crocins (coloring chemicals), about 2% picrocrocin (bitter and aromatic chemicals), 8% to 13% fats, about 13% starch, small amounts of vitamins B_1 and B_2, 0.4% to 1.3% volatile oil, numerous trace minerals, and other constituents.

In addition to being used as a domestic spice, saffron is used in perfumes, processed foods, and in alcoholic bitters and vermouths. In Western folk medicine, saffron is used as a sedative, diaphoretic, antispasmodic, emmenagogue (to promote menstruation), expectorant, pain reliever, and aphrodisiac. Conditions for which it is used include coughs, whooping cough, stomach gas, insomnia, and gout.

Effects on the body: In animal experiments, both Chinese and Western scientists have found that extracts of saffron can lower blood pressure, stimulate the uterus, inhibit action of the heart, stimulate respiration, and constrict blood vessels and bronchi.

Traditional uses: As its names imply, saffron is believed to have been introduced into China from the West, via Tibet, during the Han Dynasty, about 2,000 years ago. However, there is some discrepancy among early records regarding the identity of saffron. Saffron may have been confused with safflower in early records. Later and more accurate records estimated its date of introduction from the West to have been sometime during the Yuan and Ming dynasties (A.D. 1206–1644).

Saffron is rarely used as a spice in China. Through centuries of medicinal use, it has been traditionally considered to have the ability to promote blood circulation, dissipate blood congestion or blood clots, relieve pain and swelling, and promote menstruation. It is believed to act on the heart and liver. Conditions for which saffron is generally used include depression, tightness of chest, fright, shock, distraction (mental or emotional disturbance), vomiting blood, menstrual pain and other difficulties, blood congestion, and abdominal pain after childbirth. Long-term use of saffron is supposed to rid one of depression and tightness of the chest and to make one feel happy. It should not be used by pregnant women since it has stimulating effects on the uterus and may cause abortion.

Saffron is generally taken as a tea or decoction, but it is sometimes taken in wine. The usual daily dose is 3 to 6 g. (0.1–0.2 oz.). Saffron is quite toxic; larger doses can be fatal.

Home remedies: Due to its high cost, saffron is seldom used as a home remedy. Nevertheless, the following are three recipes taken from traditional herbals.

To treat **tightness of chest** and **abdominal discomfort** resulting from conditions such as **indigestion** and **gastrointestinal disorders** (e.g., **gastroenteritis**), a tea of saffron is used. An 18th-century recipe calls for one flower (probably three stigmas) per cup of water. After drinking the tea, one is not supposed to eat greasy or salty foods.

To treat **mental conditions** such as **distraction** and the results of **fright** or **shock,** a few stigmas of saffron are placed in one jiggerful of water and allowed to soak overnight. The liquid is then drunk.

A remedy from an 18th-century herbal for treating **vomiting blood** calls for an alcoholic infusion of saffron. One saffron flower (probably three stigmas) is placed in a jiggerful of wine (usually light wine) in a closed container. The contents are then cooked over boiling water in a covered pot for 30 to 45 minutes and the wine is then drunk.

Availability: Saffron can be bought in ethnic (especially Latin American) food stores, most spice shops, and in spice sections of some supermarkets.

SESAME

芝麻

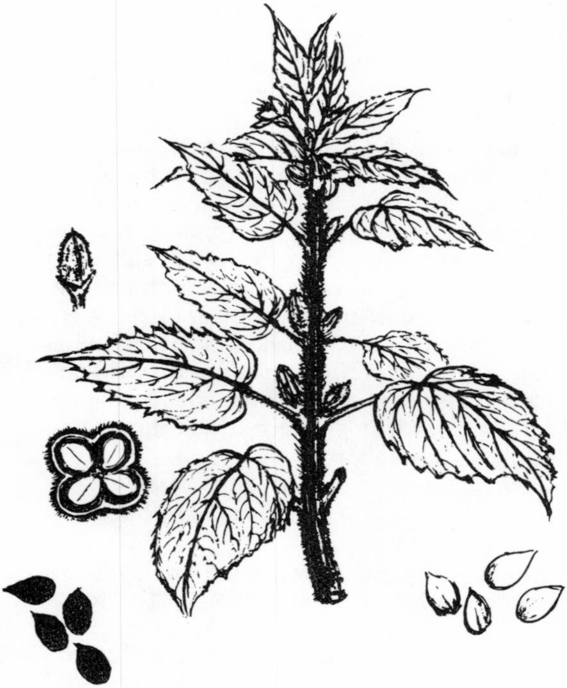

General information: Used extensively worldwide, sesame seeds are the seeds of a cultivated annual herb known scientifically as *Sesamum indicum* of the sesame family. In Chinese the sesame plant is called *zhi ma* or *hu ma,* meaning "oily hemp" or "foreign hemp." A native of southern Asia and now cultivated in Burma, China, India, Sudan, and many other tropical countries, the sesame plant is hairy and grows to a height of about 1 m. (3.3 ft.). It has an erect stem with leaves that vary in shape and size from oval to narrow and oblong or palmately three-lobed, measuring 3 to 10 cm. (1.2–4 in.) long, with petioles 1.5 to 5 cm. (0.6–2 in.) long. The plant flowers from June through August. Its fruit is a capsule containing numerous seeds. Sesame seeds are harvested during the fruiting period (August and

September) after the capsules have turned yellowish black. Whole plants are cut at their base and tied in bundles, with their tops together, and dried under the sun. After drying, the seeds are separated by thrashing, and extraneous, non-seed material is removed. Further drying yields the sesame seeds sold commercially.

Two major types of sesame seeds, black and white, are derived from the black and white varieties of *S. indicum* respectively. The small shiny seeds are smooth, oval, and flattened. They are nutritious and contain about 55% oil (fats), 26% protein, and 9% carbohydrates. They also contain vitamin E, folic acid, nicotinic acid, and minerals (especially calcium). Sesame-seed oil contains mainly oleic and linoleic acids (each about 43%), 9% palmitic acid, 4% stearic acid, and small amounts of sesamol and sesamolin.

Sesame-seed oil, also known as benne oil or teel oil, is obtained by pressing the seeds. There are two kinds of oil, one prepared from roasted, and the other from unroasted seeds. The former has a very fragrant aroma and the latter has hardly any aroma at all. Roasted sesame-seed oil is a popular condiment in Oriental foods. On the other hand, unroasted sesame-seed oil is used primarily in pharmaceuticals. It has similar properties to those of olive oil; it is used as a vehicle (carrier) in intramuscular injections and in other pharmaceutical preparations for its laxative, emollient (softening), and demulcent (soothing) properties. Roasted and unroasted sesame oils cannot be used interchangeably.

In Western countries, sesame seeds are commonly used on bread, crackers, and rolls. The white variety is generally preferred.

Effects on the body: Experiments performed over the past few decades, mainly by Western scientists, have found sesame seeds to lower the blood-sugar level but to increase the liver and muscle glycogen levels in rats.

Sesame-seed cake, obtained after expressing the oil, when used as feed, was found to be toxic to domestic animals. Calves eating too much of this sesame-seed cake were found to exhibit signs of eczema, hair loss, and itching.

Traditional uses: The sesame plant was introduced into China during the Han Dynasty, around the 2d century B.C. Its seeds have been used in traditional Chinese medicine for over 2,000 years and are first described in the Shennong Herbal, where they are listed in the nontoxic category of drugs. They are considered to vitalize the internal organs, to be particularly beneficial to the kidney and liver, and to "moisten dryness," as in treating constipation. Black sesame seeds are regarded as superior to white sesame seeds in medicinal value and are the ones customarily used in Chinese medicine. They are currently an officially recognized drug in the People's Republic of China, being listed in its pharmacopeia for the treatment of dizziness, blurred vision, and tinnitus (imaginary roaring noise) resulting from anemia, premature graying of hair, loss of hair after an illness, and constipation. Other uses recorded in traditional herbals include the treatment of lack of milk in nursing women, rheumatoid arthritis, paralysis, and general weakness after an illness. Sesame seeds are also used externally to treat insect bites, sores, and hemorrhoids. The normal daily internal dose is 9 to 15 g. (0.3–0.5 oz.), taken as a decoction, pills, or powder. Externally, a decoction of the seeds is used to wash affected areas or the mashed seeds are applied directly.

Internal use of sesame seeds should be avoided by individuals with spleen problems and by those who have loose stools.

Home remedies: Although many recipes using sesame seeds for a wide variety of conditions can be found in traditional and modern herbals, by far the most common uses of the seeds in Chinese homes are as **nutrients, tonics,** and **laxatives.** All three effects can be obtained from a drink (perhaps more appropriately called a soup) made from sesame seeds and rice. When I was growing up in Hong Kong, my family would occasionally make this soup to treat constipation in one of us, as well as for the rest of the family. We children ate the soup because it tasted good. It is prepared the same way as "almond milk" (see Almonds), replacing the almonds with sesame seeds. Like almond milk, the consistency of sesame-seed soup varies, depending on the amount of rice and water used. This soup is often prepared by the Cantonese in Hong Kong during dry weather to soothe and lubricate internal organs, particularly the bowels.

In a recipe from an 8th-century herbal for treating **aching limbs** accompanied by **swelling,** five parts of sesame seeds are heated to remove excess water, ground, and mixed with one part of wine. After soaking overnight, the wine is drunk as needed.

In the same herbal, a recipe for treating **kitchen burns** and **scalds** calls for grinding sesame seeds into a paste and applying it to the affected areas. This paste can also be used for treating **insect bites,** especially **spider bites.**

To treat **toothache** with **swollen gums,** a 4th-century recipe calls for boiling one part of sesame seeds in two parts of water until one part of liquid remains. The liquid is then used for gargling. It is said to work wonders.

According to a recipe from an early 15th-century herbal, **sores on the head and facial areas** can be treated by simply chewing raw sesame seeds and applying the resulting wet mash to the sores.

According to Li Shizhen's *Ben Cao Gang Mu,* to **increase milk**

flow in nursing mothers, sesame seeds are roasted, ground, and eaten with a small amount of salt.

Li Shizhen also gives a remedy for swollen and painful **hemorrhoids:** Boil sesame seeds in water and use the liquid to wash the affected area.

To treat **unhealing sores** and **carbuncles,** black sesame seeds are roasted well and ground to a paste which is applied directly to the sores or carbuncles as a poultice. This recipe is from a 7th-century herbal.

Availability: Sesame seeds are readily available in grocery stores and supermarkets.

SHEPHERD'S PURSE

荠菜

General information: Shepherd's purse is considered a weed in many parts of the world. Scientifically, it is called *Capsella bursa-pastoris* of the mustard family. In Chinese it is known as *ji cai.* An herbaceous annual or biennial, it has a long white taproot and erect stems that are often branched near the top, reaching a height of about 40 cm. (16 in.). Its basal leaves are deeply cut and featherlike, arising in a rosette from ground level, while its cauline (stem) leaves are lance-shaped, with their bases clasping the stems. It flowers most of the year and its fruits (capsules, called silicles) are shaped like inverted, compressed triangles, each holding 20 to 25 small seeds. The shape of the fruits resembles that of leather pouches once carried by European shepherds, hence the name "shepherd's purse."

Shepherd's purse is a native of Europe and Asia and is believed to have been introduced to North America from Europe by early European settlers. It now grows wild in fields, waste places, and roadsides in most of Europe, North America, and China. It is cultivated in China as a medicinal crop.

Shepherd's purse has been the subject of many chemical investigations. It has been shown to contain many biologically active chemical compounds, including choline (about 0.2%), acetylcholine, various plant acids, amino acids, sugars, flavonoids, sinigrin (see Mustard), saponins (foam-forming glycosides), and sitosterol. According to analyses by the Chinese Central Institute of Health, shepherd's purse herb (considered a food plant) also contains 4.24% protein, 0.32% fats, 4.8% sugars, 1.12% crude fiber, minerals (e.g., 0.34% calcium, 0.06% phosphorus, and 0.005% iron), and vitamins (especially A, B, and C).

In Western folk medicine, shepherd's purse has been used for centuries in treating both internal and external bleeding problems, including excessive menstruation.

Effects on the body: Experiments performed by both Western and Eastern scientists over the past 50 years have shown shepherd's purse to have a wide range of biological effects on laboratory animals as well as on humans. Those most extensively verified were the ability of its extracts to stop bleeding, contract the uterus, and lower blood pressure. Thus, the long use of shepherd's purse as a hemostatic in folk medicine does indeed have a scientific rationale.

Traditional uses: The use of shepherd's purse in Chinese medicine was first recorded early in the 6th century. For medicinal purposes, the whole herb is dug up in early spring; after it is washed to remove dirt and sand, it is dried under the sun.

Traditionally, shepherd's-purse herb is considered sweet-tasting and to have normalizing properties. It is said to benefit the spleen, brighten vision, promote urination, and stop bleeding. It is used in treating dysentery, edema, urinary disorders, milky urine (chyluria), spitting blood, uterine bleeding, bloody stool, excessive menstruation, and painful, bloodshot eyes. The usual internal daily dose is 9 to 16 g. (0.3–0.6 oz.) taken in the form of a decoction, pills, or powder; when using the fresh herb, 31 to 62 g. (1.1–2.2 oz.) are taken as a decoction. Externally, the powdered or mashed herb is applied directly to affected parts.

Like the herb, shepherd's-purse seed is considered in Chinese medicine to taste sweet and to have normalizing properties. It is said to brighten vision as well. However, its major use is in treating eye conditions, such as eye pain, glaucoma, and nebula (cloudy cornea).

According to a 10th-century herbal, shepherd's-purse seed "brightens vision, clears nebula, and detoxifies. Long-term ingestion makes one see objects clearly." The usual internal daily dose is 9 to 16 g. (0.3–0.6 oz.) taken as a decoction.

Shepherd's-purse flowers are used to treat dysentery and uterine bleeding. The usual daily internal dose is 9 to 16 g. (0.3–0.6 oz.) taken in the form of a decoction or powder.

Modern uses: Although most of the other medicinal uses of shepherd's purse date back centuries (some as far back as the 6th century), its use for preventing or treating measles in children is of very recent origin. Moreover, the effectiveness of this new use has recently been verified in a modern clinical setting. According to a 1970 report from Jiangsu Province in eastern China, the herb was used successfully in preventing measles. A heavy decoction was prepared from 1,000 g. (2.2 lb.) of fresh whole herb and 1,000 g. of water, boiled down to 500 g. Of 150 children who took the decoction, only seven got measles. In contrast, of 130 children who did not take the decoction, 56 got measles.

Home remedies: Numerous remedies using shepherd's purse can be found in classical as well as modern herbals. Most of these, especially those in older herbals, are very complicated. The following are a few of the simpler ones recorded in herbals of relatively recent origin.

To treat **dysentery,** a recipe from a modern herbal calls for quickly charring the surface of shepherd's-purse leaves and taking them ground and mixed with honey and water. Another recipe, from another herbal, calls for 62 g. (2.2 oz.) fresh whole herb taken as a decoction.

To treat acute **bloodshot eyes** with severe pain, a recipe from a 10th-century herbal directs one to use the juice expressed from shepherd's purse root as an eye-drop.

According to a recipe in a modern herbal from Fujian (a southeastern province), **measles** in children is treated by a decoction of shepherd's-purse herb. This decoction can be prepared by boiling 31 to 62 g. (1.1–2.2 oz.) of fresh herb in three cups of water; when it is reduced to about one cup, the liquid is drunk.

To treat **uterine bleeding,** a recipe from a practical herbal manual from Jiangxi (a southeastern province) calls for boiling 31 g. (1.1 oz.) fresh shepherd's-purse flowers in water and drinking the resulting decoction. Another recipe for the same condition, from another practical herbal, makes use of 31 g. (1.1 oz.) of the dried herb instead, also taken as a decoction.

To treat **indigestion, distended stomach,** and **lack of appetite** in children, a recipe from the same practical herbal directs one to boil 13 g. (0.4 oz.) of dried shepherd's-purse herb, 9 g. (0.3 oz.) of roasted malt, and 3 g. (0.1 oz.) of tangerine peel, and to drink the resulting decoction.

Availability: Shepherd's purse is available in most Chinese herb shops. Fresh shepherd's purse can be found growing wild throughout much of North America and Europe.

SOYBEAN (Soya)

大豆

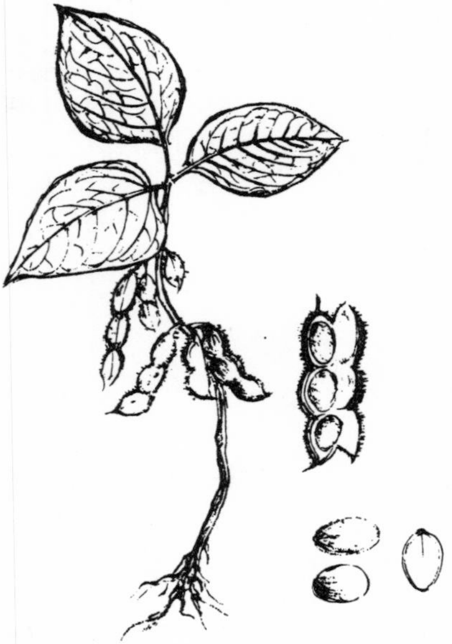

General information: Two varieties of soybean are used in Chinese medicine—black soybean and yellow soybean, known in Chinese as *hei da dou* and *huang da dou* respectively. Both are derived botanically from *Glycine max* of the pea family. (Black-soybean skin, also used medicinally, is known as *hei da dou pi.*) Black soybean has a black skin (seed coat) and yellow soybean has a pale skin.

Soybeans have been cultivated in China for thousands of years. They are a major source of protein there, mostly in the form of soybean milk, bean curd, and related products (see Bean Curd). Today they are also widely cultivated in Western countries, such as the United States and Brazil. The soybean plant is an erect, hairy annual, about 0.3 to 1 m. (1–3 ft.) tall. It produces flowers in late summer and seeds (soybeans) in autumn, with two to four seeds per pod.

Soybeans are rich in protein (up to 40%); they also contain about 18% oil, 33% carbohydrates, and 1.7% potassium, as well as enzymes and other biologically active substances. Traditional food products derived from soybeans include bean cake, soybean milk, soy sauce, soybean oil, and bean sprouts (see also Mung Bean) some of which are also used in Chinese medicine. Newer products derived from soybeans include soybean meal for feeding animals (cattle, pigs, chickens, etc.), monosodium glutamate (MSG) for flavoring foods, and purified protein for making imitation meat products such as bacon bits and steaks. This purified soybean protein has been highly treated by chemical and physical means so that it can be "texturized" —made into different textures or consistencies characteristic of certain meat products. When it is combined with added synthetic flavor chemicals, it is hard to tell the difference between these imitations and genuine meat products. Soybean proteins are also used in the manufacture of plastics and adhesives. In the earlier part of this century, Henry Ford actually tried, unsuccessfully, to perpetuate a line of automobiles based on soybean plastics, which were used for distributor and coil housings, lever knobs, horn buttons, window trim, gearshifts, and light-switch handles.

Effects on the body: In the past few years, several Western scientific studies have shown that yellow soybean can lower serum-cholesterol levels in both humans and animals and can prevent atherosclerosis (thickening and hardening of arteries) in rabbits.

Traditional uses: The recorded use of black soybean in Chinese medicine preceded that of yellow soybean. The former dates back at least 2,000 years, being listed in the Shennong Herbal, while the latter dates back to only around A.D. 1330 Consequently, there is much more documentation on the medicinal uses of black soybean and its derived products than on those of yellow soybean. Black soybean, black-soybean skin (seedcoat), fermented black beans, yellow soybean, and yellow bean sprout, as well as other, less common forms of soybean, are all used medicinally.

Black-soybean skin is prepared in the following manner: The beans are soaked in clean water until they germinate, or until skins separate easily. The skins are then removed and sun-dried. They are kept in a dry place, ready for use.

The first recorded medicinal use of black-soybean skin dates back to the middle of the 8th century, during the Tang Dynasty. It is said to nourish the blood, clear one's vision, and drive away disease-causing factors. It is used in treating excessive sweating, night sweat, dizziness, headache, and rheumatoid arthritis and is usually taken in the form of a decoction, with a usual daily dose of 9 to 16 g. (0.3–0.6 oz.).

There are two kinds of fermented black beans (*dou chi* in Chinese) —unsalted and salted. Although the only difference between the two is the added salt, the former is more commonly used in Chinese medicine. Fermented black beans are prepared by a complicated process that involves soaking black soybeans in a water extract of white mulberry leaves and a wormwood herb (e.g., *Artemisia annua*), followed by steam-cooking and spontaneous fermentation. Other herbs such as licorice and *Ephedra sinica* (*ma huang,* in which ephedrine was first discovered) are also used.

The first recorded use of fermented black beans in Chinese medicine dates back to the early 6th century, during the Liang Dynasty. It is considered bitter-tasting and is said to be good for treating illnesses that affect the lungs and the digestive system. It is used in treating colds, fevers, typhoid, headache, and discomforts in the chest. For these illnesses, it is usually taken internally as a decoction, with a daily dose of 6 to 12 g. (0.2–0.4 oz.).

Yellow soybean is considered to have the same medicinal nature as black soybean and is used in treating similar conditions.

Yellow bean sprouts are prepared by keeping yellow soybeans under wet and warm conditions until they germinate and the sprouts reach about two inches in length. Although practically unknown to most Westerners, yellow bean sprouts are a common vegetable in the Chinese diet. They taste different from mung-bean sprouts, the latter being the bean sprout most Westerners find in Chinese dishes.

Modern uses: The use of yellow soybean in the successful treatment of long-term leg ulcers was described in 1951 in a medical journal from northeastern China. According to this report, yellow soybeans were washed with warm water and partially cooked in water. After being stirred to separate and remove the skins, the beans were mashed to form a paste to which preservative was added. The ulcer was wiped clean and the bean paste was placed on a piece of thick gauze and applied directly to the ulcer. The medication was changed once a day. This treatment was used on four patients who had had leg ulcers for one-and-a-half to 12 years. All were healed after this treatment. This application was based on a traditional remedy.

An application of yellow bean sprout for treating the common wart was reported in 1963 in a regional medical journal from southeastern China. Patients under treatment were fed only plain, water-boiled yellow bean sprouts, without salt or other seasoning, three times a day. No other foods were allowed until the fourth day, when patients resumed their normal diet. All four patients treated were cured and their warts did not reappear.

Home remedies: There are many recorded remedies using soybean and, as in keeping with traditional practice, most of them contain more than one herb. Nevertheless, there are some remedies that call for soybean alone. Thus, for treating hot-water or fire **burns** and

erysipelas (an acute bacterial disease marked by fever and severe skin inflammation), black beans are cooked in water and the concentrated liquid is applied directly to the affected areas of the skin. Wounds are said to heal with no scars. To **treat poisoning due to drugs** such as croton and arsenic, boiled black-soybean juice is taken internally; sometimes the beans are boiled with licorice to enhance their detoxifying effects. Incidentally, croton oil was an official drug (as a purgative) in the United States up to 1947, when it was discarded as being too dangerous. Nevertheless, croton seed and croton oil are still used in Chinese medicine as they have been for thousands of years (both are described in the Shennong Herbal) for treating numerous disorders.

For treating a common condition characterized by **dry mouth, sore throat, dry cough,** and **constipation,** the following common home remedy is used: About four pounds of yellow bean sprouts are cooked in plenty of water for four to five hours and the liquid is taken as a drink.

Availability: Yellow soybeans are available in health food stores, groceries, Chinese groceries, and some supermarkets. Black soybeans, fermented black beans, and yellow soybean sprouts are available in Chinese groceries.

STAR ANISE

八角

General information: Star anise is better known as a spice than as a medicine. It has a flavor and aroma very similar to that of its Western counterpart, the anise seed, except perhaps a little sharper. The two spices come from completely different plant sources. Anise seed is small, the size of a grain of rice, and comes from a small annual herb; star anise is much larger and is shaped like a star, up to 2.5 cm. (1 in.) across, hence its name "star anise." It is the woody seed pod (fruit) of a relatively large tree, known scientifically as *Illicium verum* of the illicium (closely related to the magnolia) family.

Star anise in Chinese is called *ba jiao hui xiang,* which means "eight-horned fennel," referring to its usually eight-pointed form. However, occasionally it has as few as five points and as many as 13. Each point actually represents a single-seeded follicle of the fruit. In China it is produced mainly in the southern provinces of Guangxi, Guangdong, and Yunnan. Star anise is also known as *da hui xiang,* meaning "large fennel" as opposed to "small fennel." The latter is the regular fennel, which is also used in Chinese medicine for similar purposes as star anise.

The tree reaches 14 m. (46 ft.) tall and grows in southern China and neighboring countries, including India and Vietnam. A native of

Southeast Asia, it likes warm humid climates and well-drained rich soil. Star anise is usually collected twice yearly, first in summer and second in winter. It is either sun-dried or dried under low artificial heat.

Star anise contains about 5% volatile oil (star-anise oil) and 22% fats, as well as proteins, resins, and other constituents. Star-anise oil contains many flavor and fragrance chemicals. The major compound (present in 80% to 90%) is called anethole, which is also the major component in anise oil and fennel oil. The smell of star anise and anise is due to their volatile oils. The two oils are so similar in flavor and aroma that they are both listed under "anise oil" in official U.S. drug and food compendia *(United States Pharmacopeia* and *Food Chemicals Codex).* Hence, in America they are used interchangeably, to mask undesirable odors in drug and cosmetic preparations, as fragrance components in toothpastes, perfumes, soaps, creams, lotions, and detergents, and in flavoring processed foods, candies (notably licorice candies), and alcoholic beverages (especially the liqueur anisette). Anise and star-anise oils are also used as carminatives, expectorants, and stimulants in cough mixtures and lozenges.

Due to the long use of anise or star-anise oil combined with licorice, especially in licorice candies, most Westerners have mistaken the anise flavor for licorice, because when they are used together, anise overshadows licorice.

In Chinese cooking, star anise is a very popular spice, used particularly for marinating or cooking sauces such as those for spicy beef, soy-sauce chicken, and other popular dishes with which many Westerners are familiar. It is also one of the five ingredients of "five-spice powder."

Star anise is said to be occasionally adulterated with Japanese star anise which is derived from a related tree, *Illicium lanceolatum* or *Illicium anisatum.* This tree is small and grows in the same general regions as true star anise, as well as in Taiwan and Japan; its leaves, root, and root bark, but not its fruit (Japanese star anise), are also used in Chinese medicine. Japanese star anise looks similar to true star anise. However, true star anise is well formed, with follicles symmetrically joined together, while Japanese star anise looks like a smaller, deformed version, with wrinkly follicles that have sharp tips curved upward. Japanese star anise also has a bitter taste. It contains the highly toxic chemical compounds anisatin and neoanisatin, which are not present in true star anise. A 10% to 15% water extract of Japanese star anise is used in China as an agricultural insecticide, especially for vegetables.

Effects on the body: Star-anise oil can cause skin allergies, irritations, or dermatitis in sensitive individuals. The culprit is generally considered to be its major component, anethole.

The alcohol extracts of star anise have germ-killing properties effective against bacteria and fungi.

Traditional uses: Star anise has been used in Chinese medicine for centuries, but its first recorded use did not appear until the 16th century. It is traditionally regarded as having warming (invigorating internal organs, especially the heart, kidney, bladder, and small intestine) and pain-relieving, as well as phlegm-dissipating, properties. Its major traditional uses are in the treatment of vomiting, lumbago due to kidney deficiency, and abdominal pain due to hernia. The usual daily dose is 3 to 6 g. (0.1–0.2 oz.), taken either as a powder or as a tea or decoction. Star-anise oil is used mainly as a stomachic and in flavoring medicines. A single dose is usually 0.02 to 0.2 ml. and the daily dose is 0.06 to 0.6 ml. (The larger dose amounts to less than 10 to 15 drops.) The oil is usually dropped into a glass of warm water, which is then drunk. Both star anise and star anise oil are currently listed in the pharmacopeia of the People's Republic of China.

Star anise is rarely used alone, but instead is generally used together with other herbs. Thus, for treating nausea and vomiting, it is often combined with ginger and clove; and for treating hernia, with almond and green onion. Certain traditional remedies using star anise also call for toxic drugs (e.g., aconite), earthworms, pig's bladder, or cannabis seeds.

Home remedies: The following are a few less-complicated traditional remedies. For treating **hernia** of the small intestine, 9 g. (0.3 oz.) each of star anise and fennel are combined with a small amount of frankincense and boiled in three to four cups of water down to about one cup of liquid, which is then drunk.

To treat severe pain due to **intestinal hernia,** one remedy calls for frying or roasting equal quantities of star anise and litchi pits in an iron or steel frying pan under high heat until both ingredients turn black. They are then ground to a powder which is taken (3 g., or 0.1 oz. daily) with warm wine. Another remedy calls for frying a mixture of two parts star anise and one part Sichuan peppercorn (a common Chinese spice) which is then ground to a powder. The powder is taken with wine (3 g., or 0.1 oz. daily).

For treating **lumbago,** star anise alone is lightly fried or roasted and then ground to a powder. One remedy calls for taking 6 g. (0.2 oz.) of this powder with wine before meals. Another calls for taking the same dose before meals with a salty soup. The salt is said to promote the effects of star anise on the kidneys. At the same time, a hot pack of roasted glutinous rice is applied directly to the affected area.

To treat painful **hernia of the bladder,** 30 g. (1 oz.) each of star anise and almonds are ground to a powder together with 15 g. (0.5 oz.) of the white part of green onions that have been dried by baking. The powder is taken (6 g., or 0.2 oz. daily) with wine and some walnuts.

Availability: Star anise is available in Chinese groceries, in gourmet food stores, and in the spice sections of some supermarkets.

SUNFLOWER

向日葵

General information: By sunflower, we usually mean the common sunflower known to botanists as *Helianthus annuus* of the composite family. In Western countries, except for the seeds, other parts of the sunflower plant appear not to be used for food or medicine. In Chinese medicine, however, practically every part of the sunflower is used. Its Chinese names are *xiang ri kui* ("facing-sun flower") and *yi zhang ju* ("ten-foot chrysanthemum"—a reference to its height).

Sunflower is a native of America and was cultivated for centuries by native Americans for its seeds, for food. It is a tall, erect annual, up to 3.5 m. (11 ft.) high. Its sturdy stem has well-developed pith. The flower heads are large, reaching 35 cm. (14 in.) across; they are generally yellow with a brown central disk, yielding hundreds of seeds. The plant is now cultivated in many parts of the world for its seed and oil as well as for ornamental purposes. Sown in a sunny place in early spring, it will flower in summer and seed in early autumn.

Sunflower seeds (kernels) are nutritious. According to analyses by the U.S. Department of Agriculture, they contain 24% protein, 47% fats (oil), 20% carbohydrates, minerals (especially phosphorus and potassium, at 0.84% and 0.92% respectively), and vitamins (e.g., A and B). Analyses by other Western scientists also reveal that it contains simple plant acids (e.g., citric and tartaric), as well as more complex phenolic acids such as quinic, caffeic, and chlorogenic acids (see Honeysuckle). The oil contains up to 70% linoleic acid (unsaturated fatty acid), with lesser amounts of phospholipids and sterols, including sitosterol and vitamin E. The vitamin E content approaches that of wheat-germ oil. The carbohydrates consist mainly of soluble sugars (58%) and no starch.

Sunflower leaves contain sizable quantities of plant acids (9%–12% of dry weight) consisting mainly of citric, malic, and fumaric acids. They also contain chlorogenic acid, neochlorogenic acid, isochlorogenic acid, caffeic acid, and other biologically active compounds.

Sunflower pith contains phenolic acids such as quinic and chlorogenic, in addition to large amounts of sugars (53%).

The flowers contain flavonoids, triterpene glycosides, and steroid compounds.

Effects on the body: When the phospholipids extracted from sunflower oil were fed to rats, scientists discovered that they could prevent hyperlipemia (excessive blood lipids) and hypercholesteremia (high serum cholesterol) in these animals.

After being subjected to high temperatures of 110° to 300°C (230–572°F.) and fed to rats, sunflower-seed oil was found to cause liver damage and to enhance the effects of carcinogens in rats.

When an extract of the dried whole sunflower plant was used in the form of an ointment, Indian scientists found that it accelerated wound healing.

Extracts of flowers and receptacles (see below) have been found to lower blood pressure of laboratory animals (e.g., cats and rabbits). Extracts of sunflower leaves have been shown to have antibiotic and antimalarial properties.

Traditional uses: Sunflower is a recent addition to Chinese medicine, with a history of use of not more than 200 to 300 years. Practically all parts of the plant are used, including seeds, leaves, flower heads, flower receptacles (flower heads minus florets or seeds), roots, and pith.

Sunflower seeds are used to treat bloody dysentery and carbuncles. Sunflower-seed shells are used for treating tinnitus (ringing in the ear). The usual internal daily dose is 15 to 31 g. (0.5–1.1 oz.) for the seeds and 9 to 15 g. (0.3–0.5 oz.) for the seed shells, taken in the form of a decoction.

Sunflower leaves are used as a bitter stomachic and in treating high blood pressure, with a usual daily dose of 31 g. (1.1 oz.) when dried, doubled when fresh, taken as a decoction.

Sunflower flowers are used to treat dizziness, facial swelling (edema), toothache, and to induce child delivery. Normal daily dose is 6 to 25 g. (0.2–0.9 oz.) when dried flowers are used; the dose for fresh flowers is 31 to 62 g. (1.1–2.2 oz.). They are taken as a decoction.

Sunflower roots are used for treating stomachache, urinary difficulties, constipation, traumatic injuries, gonorrhea, and hernia. Normally, 15 to 31 g. (0.5–1.1 oz.) of fresh roots are boiled in water and taken internally.

Sunflower pith is used in treating urinary disorders such as hematuria (bloody urine), chyluria (milky urine), stones, and urinary difficulties, as well as whooping cough and external bleeding. The usual daily internal dose is 9 to 16 g. (0.3–0.6 oz.) taken as a decoction. Externally, the fresh pith is mashed and applied directly over affected areas.

Sunflower receptacles are used to treat headache, dizziness, toothache, stomachache, bellyache, menstrual pain, and sores and swellings. The usual internal daily dose is 25 to 62 g. (0.9–2.2 oz.) taken as a decoction.

Modern uses: Among the various parts of sunflower used in Chinese medicine, the receptacles have attracted the most attention from Chinese doctors, both traditional and modern. Over the past decade, they have used the receptacles successfully in treating arthritis and mastitis.

In treating arthritis, receptacles harvested during the flowering period were used. They were boiled in water until a sticky mass remained, and this was applied directly to the affected joints. Of over 30 patients treated in this manner, all showed improvement of symptoms.

For mastitis, receptacles collected at the seed-bearing stage were used. After the seeds were removed, the receptacles were dried under the sun, chopped into small pieces, roasted until brown, then ground into a powder. The powder was taken three times daily, 9 to 16 g. (0.3–0.6 oz.) each time, mixed with white wine or boiled water and sugar. All 122 patients reportedly treated by this method showed satisfactory results.

Home remedies: Although sunflower is a relatively new drug in Chinese medicine, there is no lack of remedies using its various parts in treating different conditions.

To treat **bloody dysentery,** a folk remedy from Fujian Province calls for 31 g. (1.1 oz.) of sunflower seeds gently stewed in water for one hour. The mixture is taken with rock candy.

To treat **headache due to colds,** another Fujian folk remedy directs one to slowly simmer 25 to 31 g. (0.9–1.1 oz.) of sunflower receptacles in two large cups of water until half a cup remains. The resulting decoction is taken twice daily after meals.

According to a folk remedy from Jiangxi (in southern China), **pain in the penis** due to **gonorrhea** is treated by using fresh sunflower root. Thirty-one grams (1.1 oz.) of the fresh root is boiled briefly in water and the liquid taken.

A Jiangxi recipe for treating **hernia** calls for boiling 31 g. (1.1 oz.) of fresh sunflower root with water and brown sugar; the resulting decoction is taken.

To treat **stomachache** or **bellyache,** one fresh sunflower receptacle is stewed with one pig stomach and the stew eaten.

To treat **stones of the urethra or kidney,** a recipe from a modern herbal from Jiangsu Province (in eastern China) calls for use of 1 m. (3.3 ft.) of fresh sunflower pith, that is, about the entire length of the stem of a good-sized plant. The pith is slowly boiled in water down to about one-fourth of the original volume. The resulting decoction is then taken once daily for one week.

According to a recipe from Inner Mongolia, fresh sunflower pith can be mashed and applied directly to surface **cuts, bruises,** and **wounds** to stop **bleeding.**

Availability: Sunflower seeds (both shelled and whole) are readily available from health food stores and supermarkets. Other parts of the sunflower plant can be obtained from farms or home gardens.

TAMARIND

酸角

General information: Tamarind is a large evergreen tree native to tropical Asia and Africa. Called scientifically *Tamarindus indica,* it belongs to the pea family. In Chinese, tamarind is known as *suan dou* or *suan jiao,* meaning "sour bean" and "sour fruit" respectively. It has a heavy trunk; although normally 10 to 20 m. (33–66 ft.) high, it can reach 25 m. (82 ft.). Its fruit is a pod (legume) measuring 5 to 15 cm. (2–6 in.) long and up to 2.5 cm. (1 in.) broad. The ripe pod has a brittle brown shell and contains up to 12 large seeds enclosed in a brown, stringy pulp. The ripe or almost ripe pod is used as a food and as medicine.

In Western countries, tamarind pulp is widely used in Worcestershire sauce and other steak sauces as well as in other processed foods. In the Far East, it is extensively used in chutney and curries. For these purposes, the pulp is shipped to manufacturers either preserved in syrup, as is the common practice in tropical America, or in salt, as is common in the Far East. The pulp is also used by local peoples for making a refreshing drink in regions where tamarind grows.

In Western folk medicine, the fruit pulp is used as a mild laxative and in cooling fevers when made into a drink.

Tamarind contains large amounts (16%–18%) of plant acids composed mainly of tartaric acid (the acid of grapes) and malic acid, which give it its tart taste. It also contains 20% to 40% sugars and, according to analyses by the U.S. Department of Agriculture, 2.8% protein, 0.6% fats, minerals (especially potassium, at 0.8%), and vitamins (e.g., A, B, and C).

Effects on the body: Tamarind pulp has mild laxative effects on humans.

Traditional uses: Use of tamarind in Chinese medicine is of relatively recent origin, with a history of use of probably not more than 300 years. Its sun-dried pod, devoid of seeds, is what is used.

Traditionally, tamarind is considered sweet and sour and to have cooling properties. Its major uses are for cooling down in summer heat and in treating lack of appetite due to summer heat, nausea and vomiting in pregnancy, parasites in children, and constipation.

The usual internal daily dose of tamarind is 15 to 31 g. (0.5–1.1 oz.) taken as a decoction.

Home remedies: According to a recipe from a collection of herbal remedies from Yunnan (a southwestern province), a decoction of tamarind pods can be taken to prevent **heatstroke** and to treat **lack of appetite, nausea,** and **vomiting** in pregnant women, **constipation,** and **parasites** in children. The decoction is prepared by simmering 15 to 31 g. (0.5–1.1 oz.) of pods in 1.5 to 2 l. (1.5–2 qt.) of water down to about one-third to one-fourth the original volume.

Availability: Fresh tamarind pods are sold in health food stores, ethnic food stores, and some supermarkets.

TEA

茶葉

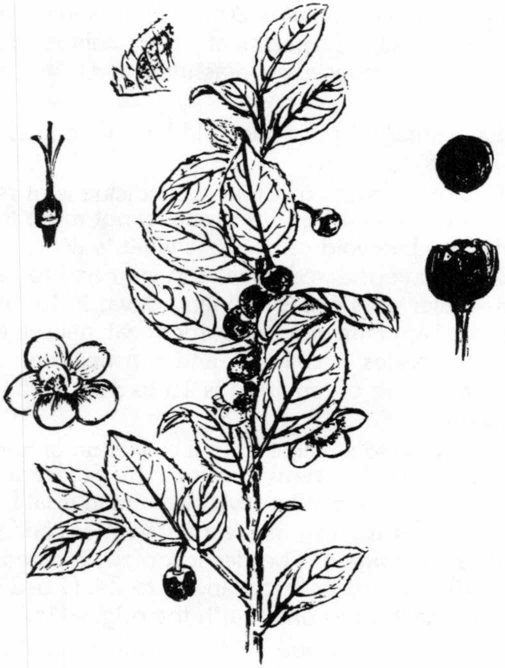

General information: Tea drinking originated in China. This custom dates back several thousand years and is now widespread in both Eastern and Western countries. The tea plant is native to the mountainous regions of southern China and India and is called scientifically *Camellia sinensis* or *Thea sinensis* of the tea family. In Chinese, tea is called *cha.* It is an evergreen shrub, or occasionally a tree, much branched, usually 1 to 6 m. (3–20 ft.) high. If allowed to grow freely, it can reach a height of 9 m. (30 ft.). To facilitate tea picking, however, the plant is pruned regularly so that its height is maintained at 1 to 1.5 m. (3–5 ft.). Tea is now extensively cultivated in China, India, Indonesia, Japan, Sri Lanka, and other tropical and subtropical countries (e.g., Kenya, Uganda, Turkey, and Argentina). There are numerous varieties, producing different types of teas.

For tea-leaf production, the leaf bud and adjacent young leaves, along with the accompanying stem, are broken off. In China, the picking is normally done three times a year, beginning early in the spring, at monthly intervals. Sometimes a fourth harvest is made early in autumn. The first picking yields tea of the best quality, while subsequent pickings yield teas of progressively inferior qualities. The tea plant is ready to be plucked three years after it is started from seed, and it continues to yield tea leaves for decades. After picking, the tea leaves are cured to furnish the teas sold commercially.

There are two basic types of tea, green and black; the latter is commonly known as red tea in China. They are produced by different curing processes. The major difference between them is in the fermentation process. Green teas are produced without fermentation and black teas are produced with fermentation. In green-tea production, after the leaf buds and leaves are collected, they are treated by steam or dry heat to inactivate the enzymes, then rolled, dried, and sorted into different grades. In black-tea production the leaf buds and leaves are allowed to wither for a day or more until they are soft enough for rolling. They are then rolled and spread out to ferment. During fermentation the enzymes present inside the tea leaves and leaf buds convert some proteins, amino acids, fatty acids, phenols, and other compounds into new compounds that give black tea a different color and flavor than green tea. India and Sri Lanka are major black-tea producers, while China and Japan are major green-tea producers.

Westerners usually drink black tea while Chinese and other Orientals prefer green tea. Over the years, tea drinking has become so popular that it has evolved into a very delicate art in some countries (especially China, India, and Japan). The true connoisseurs not only select the type and grade of tea with great care and discrimination, they also place much emphasis on the types of water (spring, well, etc.) and brewing utensils used, as well as such brewing conditions as temperature and duration.

In China and Hong Kong, there are many grades of green and black (red) tea, which differ enormously in price. The inferior grades inevitably find their way to Western countries, but at not such inferior prices. As graduate students newly settled in the United States, my Chinese friends and I found the taste of certain well-known brands of American tea bags terrible, and we used to joke about how they must have been already used in the Orient and sent to America to pass as top-grade teas. Nevertheless, these teas must taste good to many Americans or they would not be popular. On the other hand, if one grows up on chop suey and gets used to its taste, one would probably not mind eating it, especially if one has never had the opportunity to taste genuine Chinese cooking.

Both green tea and black tea contain sizable amounts of caffeine (1%–5%), which in some cases are higher than those present in coffee. They also contain large amounts (up to 27%) of tannins and related substances, fats (4%–16.5%), flavonoids (e.g., quercetin and rutin), proteins, relatively large quantities of vitamin C (0.1%–0.2%), and aroma and other chemicals, for a total of more than 300 compounds.

A strong cup of tea may contain about the same amount of caffeine as a cup of coffee, but it has a much higher tannin content, hence its puckering effect.

In Western folk medicine, the common tea bag is used as a wash for sunburn, a poultice for baggy eyes, and a compress for headache or tired eyes. As an emergency measure, a tea bag is used to stop bleeding after tooth extraction by simply placing it in the tooth socket and biting into it.

Effects on the body: The pharmacological effects of tea are due mainly to its caffeine and tannin contents. Caffeine is well known for its diuretic and stimulant properties (it acts on the central nervous system), while tannins have astringent and germ-killing, as well as both carcinogenic and anticancer, properties.

The antibacterial effects of tea have been well documented in Chinese scientific literature. Green teas have stronger effects than black teas. They are effective against many types of bacteria, including those that cause dysentery, diphtheria, and cholera.

Traditional uses: Tea's use in traditional Chinese medicine was first recorded in a well-known early 6th-century herbal, where tea is described as "good for people who sleep too much." It is considered both bitter- and sweet-tasting and to have cooling qualities. Down through the centuries, tea has been described in most major herbals as having the ability to clear one's mind and vision, remove phlegm, facilitate urination, quench thirst, aid digestion, and remove poisons from the body. It is used in treating headache, blurred vision, sleepiness, excessive thirst, dysentery, malaria, urinary difficulties, and alcohol intoxication. The usual daily internal dose is 3 to 9 g. (0.1–0.3 oz.) taken in the form of a tea, decoction, pills, or powders. Externally, tea is ground to a fine powder, mixed with an adequate amount of water and applied directly to the affected areas.

Modern uses: During the past few decades, the Chinese have been using tea preparations clinically in treating various illnesses and have reported their findings in numerous national and regional journals of modern medicine, traditional medicine, pharmaceutics, and others.

Tea in the form of a decoction was particularly effective (85% to 100%) in treating bacillary dysentery, amoebic dysentery, acute gastroenteritis (inflammation of stomach and intestine), and enteritis (inflammation of the intestine).

Furthermore, according to a report published in 1962, green tea in the form of pills was found to be effective in treating acute infectious hepatitis. Thirty patients were given 3 g. (0.1 oz.) of tea pills three to four times daily for two to three weeks. All their symptoms disappeared within 15 days; some actually disappeared as early as one-and-a-half days after treatment was started. The liver functions of the patients returned to normal after 15 to 26 days of treatment.

According to another report, published two years earlier, black tea was effective in treating hypersensitive teeth. A decoction of 31 g. (1.1 oz.) of second-grade red tea was used for gargling, and then swallowed. This treatment was used at least twice daily without interruption until conditions improved or were cured. Of 20 patients treated by this method, 12 were cured and six improved.

The major side effects of treatment with tea preparations consisted of insomnia, dizziness, heart palpitations, excessive urination, nausea, vomiting, and constipation. All these can be expected, because of the large amounts of caffeine and tannins consumed. However, Chinese are usually regular tea drinkers, and some are heavy drinkers. They have a tolerance to the caffeine and tannins in the tea. Hence, the side effects occurred mainly in those who didn't drink tea regularly or were light tea drinkers. It was also found that drinking the decoction caused more side effects than taking the pills.

Home remedies: Since tea has been used daily in China for so many centuries, there is certainly no lack of recipes using it for treating various conditions. Like other traditional remedies, however, most of them are quite complicated. The following are a few of the simpler ones.

A Cantonese home remedy for treating **hangover** calls for simply drinking a cup of strong black tea. Two or three tea bags steeped in a cup of boiling water for five to 10 minutes should make a good strong cup of tea, which should be drunk with no sugar, milk, or cream added. This same recipe is used for treating simple **diarrhea.** The tannins present in the tea are supposed to stop the diarrhea.

To treat **insect bites** or minor painful **swellings** on the skin, another folk remedy from southern China directs one to chew a small amount of tea leaves (green or black) and place the chewed wet mass directly over the affected area. This is said to stop the pain and itching, and to reduce the inflammation.

Availability: Green and black teas are readily available in Western countries. However, for fancier grades of Chinese tea (both green and red) one has to visit Chinese or gourmet specialty stores. For most medicinal purposes, the grades do not matter.

THYME

地椒

General information: Two types of Western thyme are used in Chinese medicine—garden thyme and wild thyme. Both belong to the mint family and both are natives of Europe and now grown worldwide.

Garden thyme, also known as common thyme and French thyme, is called botanically *Thymus vulgaris.* In Chinese, garden thyme is called *she xiang cao,* meaning "musk herb." It is an erect evergreen subshrub, 15 to 30 cm. (6–12 in.) high, usually with white, hairy stems and a woody fibrous root. Its leaves, hairy above, are small and lance-shaped, with no petioles (leafstalks); they measure 9 to 12 mm. (0.4–0.5 in.) long and 4 mm. (0.2 in.) wide. This thyme is cultivated extensively in European countries (e.g., Britain, France, Greece, Portugal, and Spain) and the United States, especially in California. It is also grown in China to a limited extent. Garden thyme usually contains about 1% of a volatile oil (thyme oil) that is composed mainly of thymol and carvacrol, along with minor amounts of many other aroma chemical compounds. Its other chemical constituents include tannins, flavonoids, phenolic acids such as caffeic acid and chlorogenic acid (see Honeysuckle), and triterpene acids. Much of the cultivated garden thyme in Europe and the United States is used in the production of thyme oil. This oil is used extensively in Western countries as a flavoring agent in processed foods as well as in pharmaceutical and cosmetic products. It is also used as an antiseptic, antispasmodic, carminative, counterirritant, or rubefacient in such products as cough drops, ear drops, mouth washes, liniments, and feminine hygiene products.

Wild thyme is also known as creeping thyme and mother of thyme. It is known in Chinese as *di jiao,* which means "ground spice," probably referring to its prostrate form, and as *bai li xiang,* meaning "hundred-mile fragrance," referring to its strong aroma. Called *Thymus serpyllum* botanically, it is a subshrub and creeping perennial herb with wiry stems that are prostrate (flat) and rooting below, ascending and erect above, and up to about 15 cm. (6 in.) high. Its small leaves are egg-shaped or long and elliptical, up to 15 mm. (0.6 in.) long and 7 mm. (0.3 in.) broad, with short petioles, and hairy at the base. It grows wild in temperate regions of Europe, America, and Asia (e.g., northern China); it is also cultivated in home gardens. Wild thyme contains about 1% volatile oil with carvacrol as its major component in most varieties. Its other chemical constituents include tannins, resins, fats, and triterpene acids (e.g., ursolic acid). It is much less frequently used commercially than garden thyme in Western countries.

Both garden thyme and wild thyme have been used in Western folk medicine for centuries to treat acute bronchitis, laryngitis, whooping cough, chronic gastritis, diarrhea, and lack of appetite. Infusions of wild thyme are said to be useful in breaking the alcohol habit.

Effects on the body: The biological effects of garden thyme and wild thyme are generally considered to be due to thymol and/or carvacrol. Both of these phenolic compounds have antibacterial and antifungal as well as antispasmodic, carminative, and expectorant properties, with thymol being the stronger acting. They also have anthelmintic (antiparasitic) effects, particularly against hookworms.

Both thymol and carvacrol are irritant to the skin and when ingested by accident can cause nausea, vomiting, stomachache, headache, dizziness, convulsions, coma, and cardiac and respiratory collapse.

Traditional uses: Garden thyme is a very recent addition to Chinese medicine, with a history of use of probably not more than 100 years. In fact, it is so new to Chinese medicine that its properties (which are usually determined after generations of use) have not been established. Conditions for which garden thyme (whole herb) is used include coughs (especially whooping cough), acute bronchitis, laryngitis, and hookworms. It is taken internally as a decoction with a usual daily dose of 3 to 6 g. (0.1–0.2 oz.).

Wild thyme has a much longer history of use in Chinese medicine, having been first described in an 11th-century herbal. Traditionally, it is said to taste pungent and to have warming and mildly toxic qualities. It invigorates the body, dispels colds, and stops pain. The whole herb is collected in summer and is used fresh or after drying in the shade. It is used in treating nausea, vomiting, bellyache, diarrhea, abdominal distention, headache, coughs (e.g., whooping cough), colds, body aches, indigestion, and inflammations (e.g., pharyngitis and laryngitis). The usual daily internal dose is 9 to 13 g. (0.3–0.4 oz.) taken as a decoction, wine, or powder. Externally, the decoction is used to wash affected areas or the powder is applied directly as a wet mash.

Modern uses: In recent years, wild thyme has been used clinically in China for treating arthritis and rheumatoid arthritis, reportedly with considerable success.

Home remedies: Most of the recorded recipes using wild thyme are from modern herbals from the central and northern provinces of China. A few of these are reproduced here.

To treat the **common cold** or **whooping cough,** a decoction of 3 g. (0.1 oz.) of dried wild thyme is drunk daily for a few days to a few weeks.

To prevent **heatstroke** or the **common cold,** a tea prepared from wild thyme is used daily over the period during which the patient is likely to be susceptible.

For treating **indigestion** and **stomachache,** 9 g. (0.3 oz.) of dried wild thyme is boiled in water and the resulting decoction taken.

A wild-thyme wine for treating **traumatic injuries** that cause the whole body to ache can be prepared as follows: 31 to 62 g. (1.1–2.2 oz.) of dried wild thyme is soaked in 500 ml. (1 pint) of white wine for 24 hours. The resulting wine is taken twice daily, two to three jiggers each time.

To treat chronic **eczema** and **itchy skin,** a decoction prepared from 16 g. (0.6 oz.) of dried wild thyme and 31 g. (1.1 oz.) of dandelion herb is used to wash affected areas.

Availability: Dried wild-thyme herb is available from Chinese herb shops. Dried garden thyme is a common spice, available from supermarkets or grocery stores. Fresh garden thyme and wild thyme can be obtained from home gardens.

TURMERIC

姜黄

General information: Also known as curcuma and Indian saffron, turmeric is a common spice used worldwide, being an ingredient in curry, prepared mustard, pickles, and other well-known food products. It is more often used for its yellow coloring effects than for its flavor, especially in Western countries. Turmeric is derived from the rhizome (underground stem) of a plant of the ginger family known scientifically as *Curcuma longa* or *Curcuma domestica.* Its Chinese name is *jiang huang,* or "ginger yellow," and it is also known as *huang jiang,* "yellow ginger." The plant is a perennial herb with a thick rhizome from which large oblong leaves arise. The leaf blades measure 30 to 45 cm. (12–18 in.) long and 10 to 20 cm. (4–8 in.) broad, with petioles sometimes as long as the blades. The turmeric plant is a native of southern Asia but is now extensively cultivated in many tropical countries, including India, China, Indonesia, Haiti, and Jamaica. To produce turmeric, the rhizomes are dug up at the end of the growing season, which is usually in the fall or winter. They are washed, thoroughly boiled, and dried under the sun. The rootlets and outer skin are removed and again dried under the sun, yielding the turmeric sold commercially. Two forms, "bulbs" and "fingers," are usually sold; the former is derived from the main rhizomes, while the latter is from branched rhizomes. India is the major producer of turmeric.

Turmeric contains 4% to 5% volatile oil, highly variable amounts (0.3%–5.4%) of a yellow pigment called curcumin, large amounts (65%) of carbohydrates (including 28% glucose and 12% fructose), about 8% protein, 10% fats, 6.7% fiber, minerals (it is especially high in potassium—2.5%), and vitamins (especially C). The volatile oil is composed mainly of turmerone (about 60%), zingiberene (about 25%), and numerous other volatile chemical compounds.

Although widely used as a coloring agent and spice in the West, turmeric is seldom used there as a medicine. Its primary medicinal use has been as a stimulant.

Effects on the body: During the past three decades, scientists both in China and in Western countries (especially Russia) who have tested turmeric on animals have found it to promote bile secretion, increase appetite, lower blood pressure, alleviate pain, stimulate the uterus, and reduce inflammation and edema, among others effects. Turmeric has also been shown to have antibiotic and insecticidal properties.

In a recent study reported in China, both water and petroleum-ether extracts of turmeric were shown to be 100% effective in preventing pregnancy in female rats.

Traditional uses: Tumeric's use in traditional Chinese medicine was first recorded in the middle of the 7th century. It has since been described in most major herbals and is currently listed as an official drug in the pharmacopeia of the People's Republic of China.

Turmeric is considered to have the ability to remove blood stasis, promote and normalize energy flow in the body, and relieve pain. It is said to act on the spleen and liver. Its major uses are in treating chest and rib pain, amenorrhea, abdominal mass, traumatic injuries, swelling, and carbuncles. Other uses include the treatment of hematuria (bloody urine), pain and itching of sores and ringworms, toothache, colic, flatulence, and hemorrhage. The usual daily internal dose is 3 to 9 g. (0.1–0.3 oz.) taken in the form of a decoction, pills, or powders. When used externally, the powder is normally applied directly to the affected area as a poultice.

Home remedies: Numerous recipes using turmeric for treating various conditions are recorded in classical and modern herbals. All except one call for at least three to over a dozen other traditional drugs. The following is a recipe from the 7th century.

For treating **pain** and **itching** resulting from **sores** or **ringworms,** turmeric is mashed in water and the mash is applied directly to the affected areas.

Availability: Turmeric, usually in powdered form, is sold as a spice or coloring agent in grocery stores and supermarkets.

WALNUT

胡桃

General information: Despite its name, the English walnut, as it is known, is not a native of England. Its other name, Persian walnut, gives a better indication of its origin, which is believed to have been western Asia. It is now cultivated in Europe, China, the United States, and many other parts of the world. Scientifically, it is known as *Juglans regia* of the walnut family. It is different from the black walnut *(Juglans nigra),* a native American species.

English walnut was introduced into China from the Middle East during the Han Dynasty some 2,000 years ago, and is known in Chinese as *hu tao,* meaning "foreign peach." It is a deciduous tree that can reach about 30 m. (100 ft.) high. Its fruit, 3 to 5 cm. (1.3–2 in.) in diameter, consists of a fleshy outer layer and a large pit, which yields the familiar walnut.

Like other seed or nut products, walnut is rich in unsaturated fats (usually 50%–70%), proteins (about 15%), and carbohydrates (10%–15%). It also contains minerals (e.g., potassium, calcium, phosphorus, and iron), vitamins (e.g., B_2 and A), and other biologically active constituents. Walnut has long been considered to be a nutritious food by both Easterners and Westerners. The leaves of the walnut tree and the shells of the nuts, as well as the meat itself, are made into extracts and used by the food industry in flavoring alcoholic and nonalcoholic beverages, ice creams, candy, and baked goods.

Effects on the body: Although commonly eaten as a nutritious food, walnut has occasionally caused problems for some sensitive individuals. Thus, in an editorial published in the *British Medical Journal* in 1974, recurrent oral ulceration was correlated with the ingestion of English walnuts.

Traditional uses: The first recorded use of the English walnut in Chinese medicine dates back to the early part of the 8th century. In an herbal for diet therapy of that period, its effects are described as "promoting circulation, darkening one's hair, and making one's flesh smooth and delicate if eaten often." In another herbal of about the same period, the eating of walnut is described as "making one gain weight." This does not mean one will get fat. It simply means that walnut is nutritious. Over the centuries, the medicinal uses of walnut have been expanded and documented in most major herbals, including Li Shizhen's *Ben Cao Gang Mu.* In addition to the nut itself, walnut oil, the shells, leaves, and other parts of the walnut tree are also used medicinally.

Traditionally, walnut is considered to invigorate the body, benefit the kidneys and lungs, lubricate the intestines, and strengthen semen. Its major uses include the treatment of coughing, wheezing, backache, weakness in the legs, nocturnal emission (wet dreams), impotence, constipation, urinary stones, excessive urination, and skin sores and boils.

The usual internal daily dose of walnut is 9 to 15 g. (0.3–0.5 oz.) taken plain or as a decoction. For external use, it is mashed and applied directly to affected areas.

Walnut oil, obtained by pressing the walnut meat, is used internally as a laxative and to treat tapeworm; externally, it is used for ringworm, frostbite, and armpit odor. Its usual internal daily dose is 9 to 19 g. (0.3–0.7 oz.) taken warmed. For external use, it is painted or brushed directly onto the affected areas.

Modern uses: In recent years, clinical reports on the effectiveness of walnut in treating numerous conditions have appeared in Chinese medical journals. Conditions reported to have been successfully treated include urinary stones, dermatitis, eczema, and abscesses of the external ear canal.

Results of the successful use of walnut in treating urinary stones (e.g., kidney and bladder stones) appeared to be the most consistent. These were published between 1957 and 1961 in four reports, two in the *Chinese Journal of Surgery* and the others in regional medical journals from two different provinces. According to the reports, 125 g. (4.4 oz.) of walnut meat was deep-fried in a vegetable oil until crisp. The meat was then mixed with an adequate amount (1–2 oz.) of sugar and ground to a milky or pastelike consistency. This milk or paste was eaten by the patient over a period of one to two days. For children, lesser amounts were used. After the patients took this remedy, their symptoms generally improved in a few days. The stones partially dissolved, turned soft, and were excreted in the urine, which had turned milky. Urinary stones are usually painful. In the West, we generally resort to surgery. In Chinese medicine, however, walnut is one of many remedies for treating this condition. Use of walnut certainly appears to be innocuous and it would not hurt to try it before undergoing more drastic treatment.

Home remedies: The herbals record many remedies using walnut. As is traditional, it is often combined with other herbs. A few simple examples are quoted here.

In his famous herbal, Li Shizhen describes the following remedy for treating **coughing** with **excessive phlegm:** Before going to bed, chew together three pieces of walnut and three slices of fresh ginger and swallow them, followed by two or three swallows of warm liquid or broth. Repeat the process once and go to bed. Cough and phlegm will disappear by the next morning.

To treat **acid stomach,** simply chew a few pieces of walnut until they are completely mashed and swallow them.

For treating **ringworm** or **mite infestations,** boil a few cracked walnut shells in a cup of water until it is down to about half a cup. Use the liquid to wash the affected areas.

For **excessive urination,** boil a few walnuts (meat) in water, and chew and swallow the walnuts with the aid of some warm wine before retiring.

Availability: Walnuts are available in supermarkets and groceries, either shelled or with shells intact.

WATERCRESS

西洋菜

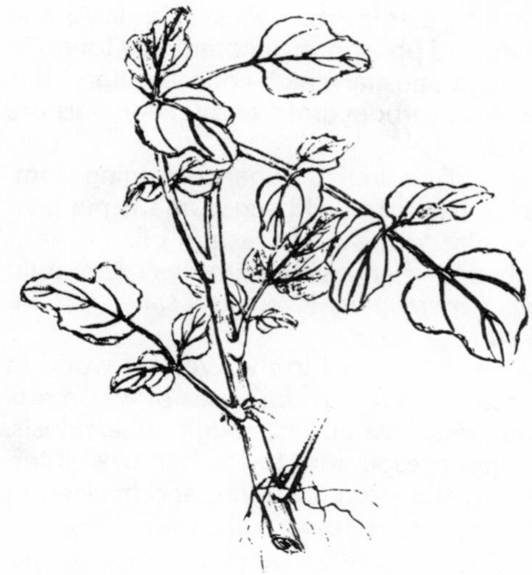

General information: Generally considered to be a native of Europe, watercress is now cultivated in many parts of the world including America and Asia. It is a perennial creeping or floating plant known scientifically as *Nasturtium officinale* of the mustard family. In Latin, *nasi tortium* means "distortion of the nose," referring to the pungent qualities of fresh watercress. A relative newcomer to China, watercress is known there as *xi yang cai,* or "American vegetable." The hollow branching stems extend 30 to 60 cm. (1–2 ft.) from the rootstock, with leaves above water. It likes cool running water and can be found growing in streams and ditches. I have frequently come across it in the Sierras of California, and once I even found a patch of it growing in a small stream halfway down the Grand Canyon.

Western herbalists generally consider watercress to be a good source of vitamin C, and fresh watercress does contain about twice the amount of vitamin C present in fresh oranges or cabbages. However, its vitamin C content is no more than that present in broccoli, cauliflower, mustard greens, sweet peppers, and many other vegetables. In order to benefit from its vitamin C content, one would have to eat more raw watercress than herbalists recommend. Furthermore, the pungent taste of raw watercress and the ensuing irritation to the mouth and throat would usually prevent people from eating enough to benefit from its vitamin C content. And since much of the vitamin

C is destroyed during cooking, cooked watercress is not a good source of vitamin C either.

Raw watercress also contains other vitamins (e.g., vitamin A) and minerals (e.g., iron, potassium, and phosphorus) commonly found in green vegetables, though none in unusually high concentrations. It is about 93% water, and its protein, carbohydrate, and fat contents are 2%, 3%, and 0.3% respectively.

Watercress also contains a glycoside (a sugar-containing compound) which breaks down in water to yield sugar and a pungent chemical with effects very similar to those of mustard oil.

Watercress has a pungent taste when raw but it tastes rather mild after it is cooked. Westerners generally eat it raw in a salad, but the Chinese usually eat it cooked.

For centuries, watercress has been used in the Western world in treating various conditions. Current Western folk uses of watercress include the treatment of gout, digestive upsets, cough, tuberculosis, anemia, and catarrh of the upper respiratory tract when used internally. Externally, it is used for treating skin blemishes and freckles. In all these Western folk uses, fresh watercress is called for.

Effects on the body: The fresh juice of watercress can cause blisters and contact dermatitis in some individuals, and can irritate the mucous membranes and skin. However, its pungent principle is destroyed when watercress is cooked.

Traditional uses: Watercress is truly a late-comer to Chinese medicine. It was probably not introduced until the middle or late 19th century, from America.

When railroads were being built in California, much of the labor was supplied by Chinese coolies, most of whom came from villages in Guangdong in southern China where my mother's family lived for generations. San Francisco used to be called (and still is by some old-timers) *gum san,* meaning "golden mountain" in Cantonese. Many Chinese young men were attracted by the idea of fame and fortune in faraway "golden mountain" and headed toward America with great hopes. Once they had landed in San Francisco, they were carted off to work on the railroad. Due to bad working conditions, many of them died from consumption or other causes and never made it home with their fortunes. Some of those who got home brought with them a new herbal drug. Legend has it that some of the laborers found out that the watercress growing along the streams in the California Sierra was good for their illness, consumption. They started gathering and eating it. After their ordeal and with every hard-earned cent saved, they headed home, bringing with them seeds of what they considered to be a miraculous plant.

Watercress has now been used in Chinese medicine for about a hundred years. It is widely available and popular in southern China, Hong Kong, and other areas in Southeast Asia where Cantonese live. It is considered to have heat-dissipating and detoxifying qualities. Its major uses include the treatment of tuberculosis, dry coughs, and what Cantonese consider as "hot" conditions, such as canker sores on the tongue or lips, blisters in the mouth, swollen gums, bloodshot eyes, and pain during urination. It is also used for internal hemorrhages. Watercress in Chinese medicine is almost always used cooked. Both fresh and dried forms are used.

Home remedies: Although watercress is primarily eaten as a vegetable, in soup or other dishes, it is often eaten with therapeutic intentions.

For treating **canker sores** or **blisters** in the mouth, watercress is boiled in water together with carrots to make a soup. There are no specific amounts called for, but ordinarily, for one person, about ¼ kg. (½ lb.) of each ingredient in about 2 l. (2 qts.) of water is used. The liquid is boiled down slowly to a third or a quarter of the original volume and the soup is drunk. For better results, a few senna leaves (about 2.5 g. or 0.1 oz.) are added. Senna is a laxative herb used both in Western and Chinese medicine. Its active principles, called sennosides, are used in many laxative preparations in Western countries.

To treat **dryness of the throat, dry cough,** or **excessive phlegm,** a popular Cantonese home remedy is simply to prepare a soup from watercress and pork to go with daily meals.

Availability: Watercress is available in Chinese groceries as well as in most supermarkets.

WATERMELON

西瓜

General information: One of the largest edible fruits, watermelon is eaten by people all over the world. It can weigh 45 lb. (20 kg.) or more, and its shape ranges from almost round to oblong. The plant is an annual vine known scientifically as *Citrullus vulgaris* or *Citrullus lanatus* of the gourd family. In Chinese it is called *xi gua,* "Western melon," denoting its foreign origin. A native of Africa, it is now cultivated in most tropical, subtropical, or warm regions of the world, among them the southern United States. It exists in numerous cultivated varieties and, depending on the variety, yields fruits of different sizes and shapes with sweet red, yellow, or greenish pulp or flesh.

Watermelon is quite versatile. In addition to its delicious flesh, its whitish rind is sometimes pickled and is also eaten. Its seeds, roasted, serve as a snack, especially for the Chinese around the time of Chinese New Year. Most Chinese handle one seed at a time, crack it open between their teeth, and deftly separate the shells and extract the edible part from the opened shell with their teeth. All this is accomplished in a few seconds with help from the thumb and forefinger only.

In addition to carbohydrates (about 6%), small amounts of protein (0.5%), fats (0.2%), and various minerals and vitamins (e.g., A and C), fresh watermelon pulp contains numerous free amino acids (notably citrulline), and other constituents (e.g., lycopene, a pigment also present in tomatoes).

Traditional uses: According to Li Shizhen, watermelon was introduced into China during the 10th century. Its first recorded uses in Chinese medicine date to the early or middle 14th century. Watermelon flesh, skin (with most rind removed), seeds, seed husks (shells), roots, and leaves are all used medicinally.

Watermelon flesh is considered to have heat-dissipating, thirst-quenching, and diuretic properties. It is used for cooling down in summer heat, fever, urinary difficulties, constipation, mouth sores, sore throat, jaundice, cystitis (inflammation of the bladder), and nephritis (inflammation of the kidney). Its juice is used internally to sober drunks. Externally, the flesh is used to treat skin inflammations of erysepilas (a streptococcal infection).

Used in the dried form (the skin is usually sun-dried after the rind is removed), watermelon skin has much the same properties and uses as watermelon pulp; its daily dosage is defined (9 to 31 g., or 0.3–1.1 oz.). In addition, it is used in treating high blood pressure and diabetes. Ashes of burnt watermelon are applied locally to treat mouth sores and toothache.

A traditional preparation of watermelon called *xi gua shuang,* or "watermelon frost," is used especially for mouth and throat conditions. To prepare watermelon frost, an opening is made at the stem end of a 7-to-8-lb. melon. After the removal of part of the pulp, the watermelon is filled with Glauber's salt (sodium sulfate) and the opening is plugged and sealed with a piece of the removed skin. It is hung in a well-ventilated, shaded place. After about two weeks, white crystals or "frost" will appear on the surface of the melon. These are brushed or scraped off and are stored in tightly sealed, nonmetal containers away from heat and moisture. They are used both externally, by direct local application, or internally in the form of a water solution for treating mouth sores, sore throat, and diphtheria, often in combination with other herbs.

Spontaneously fermented watermelon juice is used for treating first-, second-, and third-degree burns. According to the *Collection of Selected Traditional Remedies from Hebei Province,* the fermented juice is prepared from fully ripened watermelon pulp and juice. These are placed in a clean glass jar, tightly sealed, and allowed to stand at room temperature for three to four months. After filtering, the juice, which has acquired a sour plum odor, is ready for use. The burn is first washed with a cold normal saline solution or with cold water. A piece of defatted (specially treated) cotton is then dipped into the clear fermented watermelon juice and applied directly to the burned area, and this dressing is changed several times a day. According to the *Collection,* first- and second-degree burns will heal in a week and third-degree burns in two weeks.

Home remedies: As is typical in Chinese medicine, most remedies using watermelon contain other herbs as well. The following examples are chosen because of their simplicity.

To treat **toothache,** watermelon skin (dried) is burned to an ash and a small amount of this ash is placed directly on the aching tooth cavity. This remedy is from an early 17th-century herbal.

For a **sprained** and **aching back or side** that makes it impossible for a person to stretch or bend, dried watermelon skin is ground into a powder and swallowed with wine on an empty stomach. The dose is 14 to 28 g. (0.5–1 oz.).

To treat **mouth sores,** small amounts of ash of burnt watermelon skin are applied directly to the sores.

Availability: Watermelon is widely available from fruit-and-vegetable stands, grocery stores, and supermarkets.

Glossary

Throughout this book I have tried to avoid using terminology that sounds vague and abstract to the reader. Still, some of the terms are unique and cannot be easily substituted with English equivalents. They are explained in this glossary.

Cold *(han).* One of the four basic properties ("cold," "hot," "warm," and "cool") of Chinese herbal drugs. It is the opposite of "hot." Drugs with "cold" properties are used to treat conditions that are characterized by fevers or burning sensations.

Cool or **cooling** *(liang).* One of the four basic properties ("cold," "hot," "warm," and "cool") of Chinese herbal drugs. It is the opposite of "warm" and is related to "cold" by degree of potency or intensity. Drugs that have "cool" or "cooling" properties are used to reduce fevers and summer heat.

Decoction. Chinese medicines are usually taken in the form of a water extract. This extract is prepared by boiling the herb in water slowly for a minimum of half-an-hour to several hours in an earthen or porcelain pot. Pots made of metal, especially iron, are not used. To prepare the extract (called decoction), the herb is placed in the pot and covered completely with water plus another one-third to half as much. The mixture is then boiled gently until usually about one-third of the liquid remains. This liquid is decanted off. Another smaller portion of water is added to the partially extracted herb and boiled once more down to about one-third or one-quarter of the volume. This second extract is decanted off and added to the first to form the complete decoction. The major purpose of boiling (decocting) an herb is to extract its active principles. Another purpose is to render the toxic herbs less toxic and thus safer to use. In preparing a decoction, the initial amount of water used is not essential as long as it is sufficient to cover the herb adequately. However, the amount of herb used is important.

Hot *(re).* One of the four basic properties ("cold," "hot," "warm," and "cool") of Chinese herbal drugs. It is the opposite of "cold." Drugs with "hot" properties are used to treat conditions characterized by chills and shivering.

Neutral *(ping).* A property of Chinese herbal drugs which normalizes body functions or which is neutral and does not relieve fever ("heat") or chills ("cold").

Taste *(wei).* Five basic "tastes" are assigned to Chinese herbal drugs. They are: *xin* (acrid, biting, pungent), *gan* (sweet, pleasant), *suan* (sour, acidic), *ku* (bitter, astringent), and *xian* (salty). These "tastes" are closely associated with the properties of the drugs. Thus, for example, tonics generally have a pleasant or sweetish taste while febrifuges (fever-reducing drugs) often taste bitter.

Warm or **warming** *(wen).* One of the four basic properties ("cold," "hot," "warm," and "cool") of Chinese herbal drugs. It is the opposite of "cool" and is related to "hot" by degree of potency or intensity. Drugs with "warm" or "warming" properties are used to treat chills and shivering, as in malaria. It also means invigorating, a property capable of promoting body functions. Drugs with this property are hence also used in treating general debility.

Although the following additional terms may be found in English-language dictionaries, they are defined briefly here for the reader's convenience.

Antispasmodic. Preventing or relieving convulsions or spasms.
Antitussive. Suppressing or relieving coughs.
Carminative. Inducing expulsion of gas so as to relieve pain in the bowels.
Demulcent. Soothing substance used to relieve pain in mucous surfaces.
Diaphoretic. Increasing perspiration.
Diuretic. Increasing the flow of urine.
Edema. Excessive accumulation of liquid in the tissues.
Expectorant. Promoting the discharge or expulsion of mucus from the nose or throat.
Extract. Concentrated solution (as in water or alcohol) of essential constituents of a plant or other material. (See Decoction, above.)
Hemostatic. Stopping the flow of blood.
Hypotensive. Lowering the blood pressure.
Rubefacient. Applied externally to irritate or produce redness of the skin.
Stomachic. Stimulating the stomach.
Tonic. Agent that stimulates, invigorates, or increases body tone and builds up strength and resistance.

Bibliography

Bailey, Liberty Hyde. *Manual of Cultivated Plants.* New York: Macmillan, 1949.

Bailey, Liberty Hyde. *The Standard Cyclopedia of Horticulture.* 3 vols. New York: Macmillan, 1942.

Chen, C. R. *Encyclopedia of Chinese Drugs.* 2 vols. Hong Kong: Shanghai Publishing Co., 1962. (In Chinese.)

Cheung, S. C., and N. H. Li, eds. *Chinese Medicinal Herbs of Hong Kong.* Vol. 1. Hong Kong: Commercial Press, 1978. (In Chinese and English.)

Chinese Herbs and Herbal Recipes. Hong Kong: Commercial Press, 1970. (In Chinese.)

Chinese Pharmacopeia. Vol. 1. Beijing: People's Medical Publishing House, 1977. (In Chinese.)

Claus, Edward P. *Pharmacognosy.* 4th ed. Philadelphia: Lea & Fibiger, 1961.

Fernald, M. L. *Gray's Manual of Botany.* New York: American Book Company, 1950.

J. E. Fogarty International Center for Advanced Study in the Health Sciences. *A Barefoot Doctor's Manual.* Washington, D.C.: National Institutes of Health, 1974. (Department of Health, Education, and Welfare Publication No. [NIH] 75-695.) (Translation of Chinese text.)

Gosselin, R. E., et al. *Clinical Toxicology of Commercial Products: Acute Poisoning.* 4th ed. Baltimore: Williams & Wilkins, 1976.

Grieve, Maude. *A Modern Herbal.* 2 vols. New York: Dover, 1971.

Harris, Bea C. *Kitchen Medicines.* New York: Weathervane Books, 1968.

Hay, Roy, and Patrick M. Synge. *The Color Dictionary of Flowers and Plants for Home and Garden.* New York: Crown, 1975.

Herbal Pharmacology in the People's Republic of China: A Trip Report of the American Herbal Pharmacology Delegation. Washington, D.C.: National Academy of Sciences, 1975.

Hortus Third: A Concise Dictionary of Plants Cultivated in the United States & Canada. Compiled by the L. H. Bailey Hortorium Staff, Cornell University. New York: Macmillan, 1976.

Hu, Y. Y., and M. S. Xuan, eds. *Anticancer Herbs of Yunnan.* Kunming: Yunnan People's Press, 1982. (In Chinese.)

Hume, Edward H. *Doctors East Doctors West: An American Physician's Life in China.* New York: Norton, 1946.
Jiangsu Institute of Modern Medicine. *Encyclopedia of Chinese Drugs.* 3 vols. Shanghai: Shanghai Scientific and Technical Publications, 1977. (In Chinese.)
Krochmal, Arnold, and Connie Krochmal. *A Guide to the Medicinal Plants of the United States.* New York: Quadrangle, 1975.
Leung, Albert Y. *Encyclopedia of Common Natural Ingredients Used in Food, Drugs and Cosmetics.* New York: Wiley-Interscience, 1980.
Lewis, Walter H., and M. P. F. Elvin-Lewis. *Medical Botany: Plants Affecting Man's Health.* New York: Wiley-Interscience, 1982.
Li, S. Z. *Ben Cao Gang Mu ("Herbal Systematics").* Reprinted. 6 vols. Hong Kong: Commercial Press, 1977. (In Chinese.)
Liu, F., and Y. M. Liu. *Chinese Medical Terminology.* Hong Kong: Commercial Press, 1980.
Lu, K. S. *Encyclopedia of Chinese Drugs and Their Chemical Constituents.* Hong Kong: Shanghai Press, 1955. (In Chinese.)
Lu, S. *Chinese Drugs in the West.* Hong Kong: Deli Book Co., 1978. (In Chinese.)
Lust, John B. *The Herb Book.* Sini Valley, Calif.: Benedict Lust, 1974.
Marsh, A. C., et al. *Composition of Foods: Spices and Herbs. Raw, Processed, Prepared.* Washington, D.C.: Agricultural Research Service, U.S. Department of Agriculture, 1977. (Agriculture Handbook No. 8-2.)
Martindale: The Extra Pharmacopoeia. London: Pharmaceutical Press, 1977.
The Merck Index: An Encyclopedia of Chemicals and Drugs. 9th ed. Rahway, N.J.: Merck, 1976.
Mitchell, J., and A. Rook. *Botanical Dermatology: Plants and Plant Products Injurious to the Skin.* Vancouver, B.C.: Greengrass, 1979.
Morton, J. F. *Major Medicinal Plants: Botany, Culture, and Uses.* Springfield, Ill.: Thomas, 1977.
Nanjing College of Pharmacy. *Chinese Herbal Drugs.* 3 vols. Nanjing: Jiangsu People's Press, 1976. (In Chinese.)
Nanjing Pharmaceutical Institute. *Materia Medica.* Hong Kong: Shaohua Society for Cultural Services, 1960. (In Chinese.)
Polunin, Oleg, and B. E. Smythies. *Flowers of South-West Europe.* London: Oxford University Press, 1973.
Practical Herb Manual. Hong Kong: Commercial Press, 1971. (In Chinese.)
Rose, Jeanne. *The Herbal Body Book.* New York: Grosset & Dunlap, 1976.

Rosengarten, Frederick, Jr. *The Book of Spices.* Wynnewood, Pa.: Livingston, 1969; paperback, New York: Jove, 1973.

Shangguan, L. P. *History of Chinese Medicine.* Hong Kong: Xinli, 1974. (In Chinese.)

The Shennong Herbal. Reprinted. Taipei: Five Continent, 1977. (In Chinese.)

Terrell, E. E. *A Checklist of Names for 3,000 Vascular Plants of Economic Importance.* Washington, D.C.: Agricultural Research Service, U.S. Department of Agriculture, 1977. (Agriculture Handbook No. 505.)

Trease, G. E., and W. C. Evans. *Pharmacognosy.* 11th ed. London: Bailliere Tindall, 1978.

Tyler, Varro E., et al. *Pharmacognosy.* 8th ed. Philadelphia: Lea & Febiger, 1981.

Wang, B. X. *Curative Effects of New Products.* Jilin: Jilin People's Press, 1981. (In Chinese.)

Watt, B. K., and A. L. Merrill. *Composition of Foods: Raw, Processed, Prepared.* Washington, D.C.: Agricultural Research Service, U.S. Department of Agriculture, 1975. (Agriculture Handbook No. 8.)

Wu, A. B. *Encyclopedia of Herbal Pharmacology.* Hong Kong: Cheung Hing, n.d. (In Chinese.)

Wu, J. J., and C. R. Chen, eds. *An Illustrated Encyclopedia of Chinese Herbal Pharmacology.* Hong Kong: Guangxin, n.d. (In Chinese.)

Yang, J. X. *Anticancer Herbal Preparations.* Beijing: People's Health Press, 1981. (In Chinese.)

Youngken, H. W. *Textbook of Pharmacognosy.* 5th ed. Philadelphia: Blakiston, 1943.

Acknowledgments

My interest in Chinese herbal medicine dates back to my early childhood. This book is one of the results of that interest. Numerous individuals and factors have contributed to the publication of this book.

I am grateful to my maternal grandmother, who introduced me to the wonders of Chinese herbal medicine, and to my maternal great grandfather, who was the village physician and from whom my grandmother picked up her knowledge of herbs.

The illustrations of this book were done by my father, to whom I am greatly thankful. I am also grateful to my friend Lam-Kwong Sin, of Hong Kong, who five years ago sent me a copy of the then newly published *Encyclopedia of Chinese Drugs* by the Jiangsu Institute of Modern Medicine. This work rekindled and intensified my interest in Chinese herbs.

Special thanks go to my wife without whose patience and understanding this book could not have been written. She not only typed the whole manuscript but also offered helpful criticisms and suggestions. Being a Westerner, she had viewpoints that counterbalanced mine to make this book more valuable.

Index